# TEENS Encounter CHRIST

In all catechesis it is the Word of God, the person of Jesus Christ, who resounds. It is His Spirit who changes hearts, reveals needs, challenges and comforts. To the catechist is left the task of utilizing this immense spiritual force.

The Teens Encounter Christ retreat program has as its special focus the Paschal Mystery of Jesus Christ. It has the same invitation to the Good News which has always been the Christian Message. It has a clear and uncompromising presentation of perennial religious realities in a culturally sensitive atmosphere, with religious music, talks and discussion sensitive to the teenage candidates. These characteristics — exhaustively explained in the following pages — are the secret of the increasing effectiveness of the program and the best guarantee that it will continue to be a powerful influence for good in the lives of many young people.

# TEENS
# Encounter
# CHRIST

ANDRE` CIRINO O.F.M.

FRANCINE ROGERS

**INCLUDING DETAILS ON
RESIDENTS ENCOUNTER CHRIST
and
HANDICAPPED ENCOUNTER CHRIST**

**ALBA ◢ BOOKS**

The symbol on the back cover is from a painting by Michelangelo portraying a strong God in an on-going act of reaching out. We, though less determined, seek to make this encounter with God a reality.

The Authors wish to thank the Firms listed in the footnotes, or otherwise indicated, for kind permission to quote from their publications. Other Scripture quotations are from the New American Bible and used by permission.

Library of Congress Catalog Card: 77-088321

ISBN 0-8189-1156-5

© 1978, Alba House Communications

Canfield, Ohio 44406

Printed in the United States of America

## DEDICATION

*We wish to dedicate this work to*

*Sister Mary Anita Hogan, O.S.F.*

*in honor of our friendship and in appreciation for her work, support, and encouragement in the establishment of TEC in the Archdiocese of New York.*

# *CONTENTS*

# FOREWORD

"We speak like those who strive to please God, 'the tester of our hearts,' rather than men." (1 Thess 2:4)

In prayer, the Lord gave us this reading as we struggled with a very lengthy list of names of people who deserve thanks for contributing to this manual. While some contributions have been edited and other sections authored by us, we feel that the Lord is saying that gratitude should be given to the Body of Christ. If this manual could speak, it would say to the Body of Christ: "Your hands have made me and fashioned me." (Ps 119:73)

"God has so constructed the Body as to give greater honor to the lowly members." (1 Cor 12:24) In praise to Jesus, the Head, do we lift up the following members of His Body in gratitude for their particular contributions:

—Gloria Rubeo for leading the original meetings to gather people and material for this manual.

—Dan Perry for extensive use and modification of his *TEC Lay Director's Guide.*

—Father Matthew Fedewa for use of his article on TEC.

—Sam Lee for being the critical first reader and editor of the text.

—The Franciscan Province of the Immaculate Conception for supplying funds to reproduce copies of the original manuscript.

—Fathers Tom DeCarlo and Paul Monahan, our brothers in TEC at DesMoines, for use of some of their thoughts in the Progression of Talks.

—Father Charles Kavanaugh who assisted us in the early stages of publication.

—Jo De Los Reyes who painstakingly gave of her time to type the first draft of this text.

Andre R. Cirino, OFM
Francine R. Rogers

## THE PURPOSE AND USE OF THIS MANUAL

The publication of this manual has come about through the love and dedication of many people who have come to know Jesus more deeply through the TEC program.

We have compiled the manual according to the format that originated from Michigan, with the hope that it will be beneficial and useful in any place where there is a desire to initiate a TEC program.

This manual is only a guide, not a recipe for a "ready-made" TEC. It should assist the lay director and team in defining their roles and in guiding them in the preparation of their talks and meditations.

TEC is basically an experience for young people to encounter the Lord Jesus in His Word, in others, and in the Eucharist. Theoretically, we should not need a manual because the Lord, in His spontaneity, surprises us continually in so many different ways. So we issue a caution in its use: the text in no way should minimize the spontaneity, flexibility and creativity that the team must develop either before or during the Encounter. We cannot become dependent on its use, so that the TEC program becomes just another stagnant formula.

We draw the attention of the Lay Director to the sections that define his role and responsibilities in preparing for the TEC. The team members are encouraged to read carefully the section on the progression of talks in order to assist them in evaluating their talks as an essential component to the whole Encounter.

We have added two sections concerning programs that have emanated from TEC, namely REC and HEC.

*Residents Encounter Christ* (REC) is an adaptation of TEC for use in correctional facilities.

*Handicapped Encounter Christ* (HEC) is an adaptation for the handicapped.

We have also included the name and address of a resource person for both REC and HEC at the end of each section.

We encourage all—new-comers, former TECers, as well as former team members—to read as much of this manual as possible before working on a TEC. This will insure greater knowledge of the program and, hopefully, strengthen one's faith in permitting the Lord to use us in the work He has given us to do.

Roger W. Giglio, OFM

# 1
# Meeting
# the Lord

Depicting the Christian missionary images the courageous Maryknoller, Bishop James Walsh: one who desires to give away free a pearl of great price to a people who neither want it nor see the value of it. Anyone who has stood before a group of young people in a high school religion class or CCD program should be able to see themselves in this frustrating and at least sometimes humorous paradox of the missioner.

Knowing Jesus the way we do, having experienced the new life that emerges when the good news of the Gospel becomes our own good news, seeing so clearly the sore need of those who have not come to know the fulfillment that flows from the life-giving waters of a Christ-centered life, we move out to catechesis!

But, as the good news "resounds," we slowly begin to realize that our enthusiasm is not being shared. What to do?

Catechists, the resounders of the good news, have responded in a great variety of ways to what has been called the modern persecution: being ignored. Like the missioners of old they tried to discover what the "natives" *are* interested in and hold it out as a bribe.

So, for example, we gather our catechumenate in a gym: dancing, basketball—that's more like it. They might even put up with us for an hour or so once in a while in return for that!

We also had the discussion group which was a response to getting the "natives" interested. Responding to something they "liked" to do, we discussed and discussed and discussed. Unfortunately between discussion and "Superstar" the real "god-spel" became the boring prerequisite to what we really want to do.

Finally, there were those who had nothing but disdain for bribery and the "pop" approach. Refusing to "water down" or "make relevant" the teaching of religion, they held fast and endured the pain of being ignored.

Catechists today find a little of themselves in each of these categories. Though they are glibly presented here for emphasis, we all can admit that most of us are still wrestling with the paradox of the unwanted pearl.

We have grown up enough to replace the important content that disappeared from many religion programs at the bidding of "relevance." We have gained enough faith and enough confidence to free us from the fear of "losing the young people." We have learned that it is God who draws all of us to himself and we need not bribe anyone. And most of us have even learned to see the humor in our sometimes compulsive tendency to preserve the faith until it becomes something like taxidermy.

Revelation comes through culture. As Jesus used mud to heal blindness and God used myth to reveal truth, we are called to the creative use of the culture of those to whom we minister the gospel. Faith is in life, in play, in dance. It is communicated by living, breathing people—dancing, playing, and being together.

Perhaps the greatest lesson many are learning today is that in all catechesis, it is the Word of God, the person of Jesus Christ who resounds. It is His Spirit who changes hearts, reveals denied needs, convicts, challenges and comforts. To us is left the humble but essential task of being mud. God will use us, we are learning, if we are open ourselves to his loving direction.

It is this content-rich, culturally sensitive, and Christ-centered approach which characterizes the retreat program called Teens Encounter Christ. Even during the height of the above-mentioned excesses, TEC spoke soundly and maturely—in an almost prophetic way—to both young people and religious educators. In my own experience as a candidate on a TEC weekend, a team member on TEC and on the first *Residents Encounter Christ* at Greenhaven State Prison and now as a high school religion teacher, I have found TEC invaluable.

It was instrumental in my first recognizing my personal relationship with God. It was an opportunity for me to grow by serving others on TEC teams and now it is a dependable catechetical tool providing an opportunity for my students to be exposed to an honest religious experience.

The reason TEC has been so effective over such a long period of time, I believe, lies in the fact that the program has a serious and challenging focus: the Paschal Mystery of Jesus Christ. The riches of the Easter Christ event are opened to the candidate in a direct and meaningful way. There is no apology for Christ. There is the same invitation to Good News that has always been the Christian message. Because of Jesus, we are special, we are loved, we are then called to live out that unique life of love.

We are all aware of the hunger among our young people for something to rescue them from the stifling mediocrity and meaninglessness of contemporary life. TEC speaks clearly and uncompromisingly about the valuable pearl. The focal message is resounded in a culturally sensitive atmosphere. If done correctly, this awareness of the young people's interests serves to accentuate the relevance of Jesus Christ in an honest and straightforward way—like the velvet background on which pearls are displayed.

Contemporary religious music, opportunity for

discussion and criticism of the talks, peer team members both as table leaders and speakers, the ability of the team to be real enough to be themselves—all of this when present in a balanced manner sharpens the encounter's ability to speak to the people God has called to the retreat weekend.

The Easter Mystery presented in a way sensitive to the teenage candidates is only two-thirds of what makes TEC effective. The final characteristic is one which much permeate both the content and atmosphere of the encounter weekend. That all-pervasive element is a faithful dependence on God. There must be this recognition that it is God who works. He draws people to Himself. He opens hearts. He graces. He gives faith.

The TEC teams must be centered on Christ. It is this center which makes prayer the most important part of preparing for a weekend. It frees all from the fear of "success/failure" that so often plagues catechetical efforts. It provides the calm that allows one to laugh at oneself and to speak from one's heart.

I believe that these three elements—1) an authentic announcement of the Good News of Jesus Christ 2) in an atmosphere created for the lifestyle of the teenage candidate 3) by a team of Christian adults and young people who are faithfully depending on God—are the reasons for recommending the Teens Encounter Christ program as a sound and mature approach to resounding the Gospel for young people.

*Tom Rogers*
*September, 1977*

# 2
# Teens
# Encounter
# Christ

CCD Schools of Religion and the Religion Departments of Catholic high schools and colleges feel a need for a program which is an evangelistic-initiation experience of Christianity. *Teens Encounter Christ* (TEC), which its founder, Father Fedewa discusses here, is just such a program. Properly handled, TEC can be an excellent supplementary program to religious education. For in TEC, unlike many similar programs, there is a consistent, prudent, sensitive and well-informed direction.

## ORIGIN OF TEC

TEC—the word and the exercise—had its origin in the Diocese of Lansing, Michigan. The doors of TEC Lodge, 65 Emmett Street, Battle Creek, Michigan, first opened on October 9, 1965. The TEC movement, as we now know it, is an outgrowth of the Pastoral Institute of Loyola University in Chicago. It was developed and structured by Father Matthew Fedewa and Sister Concetta, R.S.M. The exercise is now conducted on a regular basis in several dioceses in the U.S. The TEC manual and TEC materials have become the basis of modified, occasional exercises in many other places.

## TEC AND YOUR PROGRAM

Religious educators have come to accept Marcel Van Caster's concept of the triple task of the catechist. His mission is not just to impart a body of objective divine truths that demand assent (*information*). It is not only that these truths have value for his hearers, that they can give new meaning to life, help solve problems or give Christian fulfillment to his personality (*formation*). It involves all this, but also much more. It means presenting the Christian message in such a way that the hearer sees it as a dynamic personal invitation from Christ, calling him to a deeper unison in faith (*initiation*).

It is also generally pointed out that there are three stages in coming from unbelief to belief: pre-evangelization, evangelization, and catechesis proper. If one is willing to think in terms of this three-fold task, and threefold stage, then TEC experience must be considered primarily initiation and evangelization.

Candidates for TEC are usually already enrolled in a religious education program whether in CCD

or in a Catholic School, where adequate time is given to the other tasks and the other stages. "TEC experiences" are not meant to *replace* other religious education programs, but only to *supplement* or *complete* them. This warning is necessary because with the introduction of TEC, some CCD directors in parishes were too quick to drop the existing program in favor of a once-a-month "experience."

The dangers inherent in this decision have been pointed out by Gabriel Moran:

> The intense emotional feelings of childhood and adolescence will pass away and this should be to our advantage. Certainly, religious teaching ought not to be played too closely into their feelings. Any kind of religious revivalism among adolescents is, I would suggest, a highly risky and doubtful business.... There is a certain kind of salesmanship of religion that plays upon young people's feelings without bringing to bear human understanding and control. (*Vision and Tactics,* Herder and Herder, New York, pp. 94-95.)

From the foregoing remarks, it should be obvious that TEC must never be isolated from total religious education.

> TEC is not a leader formation program, no more than Christianity itself is for leaders only ... TEC is not a vocation program designed to get seniors into seminaries and convents ... TEC is not a cursillo de Christianidad ... TEC is not a "group dynamics retreat" ... TEC is meant to be evangelization ... TEC is initiation .... Since TEC is a normal part of religious formation, it should be under the Office of Religious Education in the Diocese. (TEC Manual, Matthew J. Fedewa, Battle Creek, Michigan, p. 9.)

## NOT REVIVALISM

While authorities of the calibre of Gabriel Moran warn against revivalism among adolescents, other authorities of equal stature, such as Johannes Hofinger, emphasize that initiation-evangelization have a place in the normal process of religious formation of the adolescent:

> Evangelization has a place in the normal process of religious formation. Let us take the child who grows up in a good Christian family and is sent to an excellent Catholic school where the work of the family is continued and gradually completed. Everything is done well; the student loves his religion and steadily progresses in the knowledge and love of God. Yet something may still be lacking, even in such circumstances. Despite his willing response, the student may not yet have realized the greatness and the depth of his Christian vocation. He knows his religion, but he has never experienced its full Challenge; he has never been 'Shocked.' (*Pastoral Catechetics*, Johannes Hofinger, S.J., Herder and Herder, p. 156.)

Father Hofinger says that initiation-evangelization will produce "shock." He goes on to explain:

> In short, evangelization will give them a wholesome 'shock.' Shock here is not used in its strict medical sense. It merely emphasizes that the first encounter with Christ by personal faith is usually experienced by the convert as a sudden agitation of mind, when he realizes the undeserved gift and happiness of his Christian vocation.

> Every Christian should be given the great external grace of being presented with the core of the Christian message at the cross-roads of his life in a manner similar to the evangelization of mission catechetics when one is about to graduate from high school or college. (*Ibid.*, p. 156.)

It was the conviction of the founders of TEC that a young adult should have the opportunity for an evangelization-initiation experience as part of his religious education. Experience confirms this view but also confirms the conviction that the line between evangelization-initiation and revivalism is very thin and that the man who calls from Atlanta to say: "Send us the stuff, we thought we would put on a TEC this weekend for a bunch of kids," knows nothing about TEC and very little about religious education.

Every religious educator is sensitive to that choice moment that comes now for this one, and now for that one, when he feels evangelization-initiation is in order. He may do what he can for the individual, but of its very nature, the initiation-evangelization in Christianity must be a community experience.

Yet the teacher cannot presume that his particular community of students have all arrived at this privileged moment, and decide to put on a TEC experience for his class. There seems then to be no choice but for the diocese to have a TEC center, which operates continually. Here, young people from throughout the diocese can come "when they are ready" and spend a weekend with other youths their own age who have also chosen to be part of this experience at this moment in their lives.

While we speak of prudence and caution, we cannot afford to ignore this experience, feeling that initiation is a nicety that can be dispensed with as long as there is information and formation.

11

Very often, as Alfonso Nebreda, S.J. has noted, information and formation is inaccurate or inadequate until there has been initiation.

## TIME, CONTENT AND METHODS

Content and method in TEC are all of one piece.

The content of this exercise is the "good news," the core of the Christian message, the mystery of Christ—the plan of the Father to call us in Christ by the power of the Holy Spirit to a life of personal intimacy with him in the community of the Church. It is the mystery of the love of the Father in Christ, as set forth in the early chapters of the *Acts of the Apostles*. The plan of the Father has centered on the *paschal mystery* of Christ's death and resurrection. This mystery is operative now, and calling each man to conversion and life.

The central experience of TEC is the paschal mystery. The method of the exercise is the method used by the Church in its annual and weekly celebration of this mystery: *the Lent—Easter—Pentecost event* and the *Sunday experience*.

Accordingly, the exercise takes place on Saturday, Sunday and Monday. Sunday, the weekly celebration of this mystery, has been given the central place in the exercise. The "Constitution on the Sacred Liturgy" inspired this decision in its Article 106:

> ... By an apostolic tradition which took its origin from the very day of Christ's resurrection, the Church celebrates the paschal mystery every eighth day .... Hence the Lord's day is the original feast day, and it should be proposed to the

piety of the faithful and taught to them so that it may become in fact a day of joy . . . .

While the Lent—Easter—Pentecost experience is the paschal mystery experience in "slow motion," TEC is a concentrated form of the same experience. Candidates have summarized the exercise in three words: *die, rise, go.* They come, not only to hear about death, resurrection and mission in Christ, but also to experience these mysteries in a community in which Christ lives. The unity of the three-day experience was grasped by the candidate who said: "It does not seem like three days; it seems more like one day with two naps."

The mood and spirit of SATURDAY is that of Lent. Some of the objectives of the day are to achieve a sense of community metanoia of death, not for the sake of death, but for the sake of *transformation.* The method is as follows: A teenager speaks on "Ideals and Maturity." The Word of God is explained and enthroned at this time. This is followed by a Spiritual Director's talk on the "Paschal Mystery" as the death-to-life process of Christian growth.

Then there is a talk on "Penance as Sacrament of Metanoia"—the present Sacrament of transformation. This is followed by a meditation on the parable of the Prodigal Son and a personal account of Metanoia in a TECer's life. Next, there is a community celebration of the Sacrament of Penance. Saturday ends with an explanation of the "Church's Paschal Vigil" and a paraliturgical paschal vigil service in which the vows of Baptism are renewed, as in the Holy Saturday service.

The spirit of SUNDAY is that of Easter. As the

13

sacrament of metanoia is the climax of Saturday, so Sunday's objective is the sacrament of the death-resurrection of Christ, the Sunday Eucharistic liturgy. The entire day is devoted to dedications which prepare the community for an experience of the risen Christ in the Eucharist, and in the community of the Church which they have formed, though they were strangers to each other only yesterday.

Sunday begins with a meditation on the "Risen Christ." Talks are progressive, beginning with "God is a Community of Love." This is followed by the "Christian Life—Piety" talk about how we relate to God. The next talk is about the "Church as the People of God."

Communion between God and His people and among the People of God is through "Sign," the greatest of which is the "Sacred Liturgy of the Eucharist."

Following the Liturgy, former TECers come in the evening for a hootenanny, to make evident the living church as a community of joy in Christ. Having become aware of their oneness in Christ with each other, the candidates spend Sunday evening sharing their joy in "skits" and their thoughts at the present moment.

The mood and spirit of MONDAY is that of Pentecost. A meditation on "Confidence in Christ" begins the day. Our call to holiness is made by a married couple, a religious, and a single person. This is followed by the Spiritual Director's talk on the theology of "The Church in the World."

A team member, as witness to the Christian life lived, addresses the candidates on "Christianity in

Action." A TECer advises the candidates about what to expect "Beyond TEC." All participate in the Mass of the Spirit where they are invited to "go" and carry the good news to others. A renewal of Confirmation promises is the final experience for the candidates.

## WITNESS-SIGN

We encounter through signs. God has revealed Himself in Christ through four privileged signs: liturgy, Bible, systematic teaching and the testimony of Christian living. So far we have explained the doctrinal sign, the *systematic teaching* at TEC. A privileged position is given the *Scriptures* enthroned in a place of honor in the conference room. Each talk begins with a reflection on the Word of God pertaining to the current talk. The themes presented in Scripture and developed in the talks are celebrated in the *liturgical* sign: celebration of the Sacrament of Penance, paraliturgical paschal vigil service, paraliturgical renewal of Confirmation, and the Sacred Liturgy of the Eucharist.

The TEC team, consisting of a cross section of the Christian community—high school seniors, college students, adult lay persons, sisters, and priests —constitute the *witness sign.*

In regard to the witness sign, we might recall the words of Alfonso Nebreda, S.J. :

> But the word alone is insufficient. Never before, perhaps, has man been so painfully aware of the pitfalls of human words as he is now. We are confronted daily with a flood

15

*Every religious educator is sensitive to that choice moment that comes now for this one, and now for that one, when he feels that evangelization-initiation is in order. He may do what he can for the individual, but of its very nature the initiation-evangelization in Christianity must be a community experience.*

of words whose main purpose seems, not communication between man and man, but a distortion of what man actually thinks. But there is a total existential word, a word full of truth and free of all ambiguities. It is the living word of the man—his whole life, his attitudes towards things and persons. (*Pastoral Catechetics,* Herder and Herder, New York, p. 77.)

TEC has shown that a total diocesan community can participate in the formation in faith of the next generation, and in the process itself become renewed. Each TEC weekend is conducted by a different Lay Director, who in turn selects team members. It becomes a diocesan witness sign, so in the minds of the candidates TEC is not identified with any one priest, religious, or lay person. Being on a TEC team involves one in personally living out the paschal mystery in a series of advance meetings wherein people who have been strangers become a community in Christ, and who then share their death-to-life experience with the candidates.

While the teams are very effective witness signs, many times the *candidate-to-candidate witness* is the most effective. Andrew Greeley has spoken of "reverse hypocrisy" in reference to the American Catholic youth. Youth is usually good on the inside, but feels that it must appear evil on the outside.

At TEC, the candidate finds himself still in his peer group, but among candidates he has not known previously. Since his "friends," are not present, he no longer feels the need of being phony. (No more than six candidates from any one school, area, or CCD program are allowed on the same weekend; thus, only one candidate from each place is seated at each of the six discussion groups. This also allows for cross-socialization.)

## KEY IDEAS

1. The experience of a *community of Christian faith, hope and love* consisting of persons of their own peer group is often a first for many of the candidates. But to experience Christian community is really to experience Church.

2. Speakers at TEC avoid talking about teenage morals with which our candidates have been confronted for so long in the name of Christianity. TEC is *evangelization*, like Peter's sermon on Pentecost. It breaks forth with the "good news," and then waits for the echo of response. Like the man who speaks his proposal for marriage, it cannot be argued or reasoned. It calls only for a response or refusal.

3. The musical idiom of TEC is the folksong, a significant factor in *people's lives and love*. What is spoken of in the talks is sung about in songs. Each evening the exercise continues until midnight since, by habit, the candidate does most of his "real living" in the evening hours. Except for Liturgy, candidates are in casual attire, and they are permitted to smoke. Every effort is made to "let the candidate be himself."

The concept of "witness-sign" and the "key ideas" mentioned above come to TEC from the insights of early catechetical pioneers, especially Fr. Johannes

Hofinger, S.J. and from the conclusions of the Eichstatt International Study Week.

Attendance at TEC is completely optional. No school or CCD program is allowed to make any policies which would make attendance mandatory in any way. If the outcome of the exercise is to be a response of love, there must be complete freedom, for there can be no love unless there is freedom.

## TEEN PSYCHOLOGY—OTHER-CONSCIOUS

Ignace Lepp has written that a child becomes an adolescent when he becomes self-conscious. An adolescent becomes an adult when he becomes other-conscious. Many counsellors, teachers and parents have commented on the new level of maturity that the young person achieves after three days at TEC. If this maturity is real, it can only be because he has been made very much other-conscious.

Often, however, this new trust and respect for others turns to bitterness when the "other" back home takes this new love and trust and "uses" it. The words of Simon and Garfunkel come to mind then: "If I never loved, I never would have cried."

If the young person is not helped over this hurdle by his regular religious educator at home, we may find that "the last state of that man will be worse than the first."

The American adolescent living in the second half

19

of the 20th century is in a positivistic milieu. He feels that every religious assertion is gratuitous and lacks reality. More information or formation will not help him over this crisis. He needs to realize that his experience is wider than his knowledge. What he needs is an experience with the reality of himself being "in Christ" and therefore in God. He needs to become aware that this is a reality beyond human logic, but not necessarily beyond human experience.

Upon returning home from TEC he finds he is experiencing something very real, and yet he cannot find words to express what he feels.

## I IN ANOTHER

The adolescent wants to establish his own Christian identity. But he needs others to be mirrors in which he establishes his identity. At TEC, it becomes obvious that when a candidate speaks to the whole group, he is not so much speaking to them, as he is listening to himself.

Again when other candidates speak, he listens intently because so often these others, whom he has come to recognize as "real people," are verbalizing the very feelings he is aware of, but which he has never been able to express, because of his own inner doubts, confusions and fears.

But this also can lead to an abuse of openness. An adolescent who comes to regret his past may want to punish himself by a masochistic openness before a whole TEC group. This is psychologically unhealthy, and will benefit no one. Openness at TEC must mean being open to others, i.e., willing to listen to them, and openness to the Spirit of God and His inspirations. *Openness about one's own past sins is for the Sacrament of Penance, or a very close and trusted friend, not for an exhibition before a room full of peers.*


## FEAR OF CHANGE


Many adolescents fear to participate in the TEC exercise because they fear it will "change" them. Many a girlfriend or boyfriend will discourage the other from attending for fear he will "change" and "I love you like you are now." On the other hand, however, once one has attended, he will likely talk the other into attending too.

Other adolescents like the "change" they see in persons who come back from TEC, and they sign up for a weekend because they also want to get "It." And herein lies another psychological trap: To attend TEC looking for "It" is to entertain a false hope. The experience of encounter cannot be the automatic end of a weekend exercise. Though a person reaches out with all his being, he may find that his hands and heart remain empty. Besides, the uniqueness of each person prevents one from coming away with the very same experience as another.

## NO COMMITMENTS

Some candidates are afraid to participate in the liturgical experiences at the exercise for fear that "I will be phoney, because I do not know if I will still feel this way tomorrow or the next day." The TEC Book supplies this consideration: "When we act out our convictions in ceremonies, it is our conviction of that moment we are living. No one can know what his convictions will be tomorrow."

Nor is the TEC weekend intended to be a time of promises or commitments. It is intended to be a time of an evangelistic-initiation experience of Christianity. One should never give the impression that TEC is the only place where young people can have this experience.

We might conclude with these words of Gabriel Moran:

> I would be more than a little skeptical of attempts to bring on an ultimate and total commitment to Christian faith as early as possible in the lives of students. Life must be kept multi-dimensional. Christian faith cannot be inserted as the answer to their problems nor as the primary motive of their actions. (Moran, *Op. Cit.*, p. 95.)

## TEC AND FREEDOM

TEC has become the official name of this exercise since it includes all three of its important aspects: Teen, Encounter, and Christ.

> Encounter is the meeting of persons in an I-Thou relationship on the level of mutual understanding and love. Not

purely conceptual knowledge, however, rather a sort of general synthetic intuition which results not only by reasoning but by 'seeing' from the ensemble of many partial experiences and ideas. (Nebreda, *Op. Cit.*, pp. 140-41.)

God reveals himself to the candidates in Christ. The team cannot respond for him. The staff must remember that their situation is similar to the one who sets up a blind date. He provides a situation for two persons to encounter each other, and hopes they will enjoy each other's company.

At TEC there are no lectures or conferences, but talks and meditations. The greatest good we can do for another is not to give him our wealth, but to show him his own.

All attendance at TEC is to be completely optional. However, it is true that often a priest or school counsellor can assist a candidate to become "free from" peer group pressure, his own inner inertia, embarrassment for lack of money, school activities or a job.

The team is present to be the servants. The team is present to keep the exercise moving, not to impose limits on the candidates.

## CONCLUSION

Experience with the TEC exercise makes it evident that far from replacing other types of religious educational structures, it creates a need for more and better programs of information, formation and pre-evangelization, as well as catechesis proper.

Experience also shows that an evangelization-

initiation exercise can turn into an unhealthy revivalism unless there is consistent, prudent, sensitive and well-informed direction. Yet, fear of unhealthy reactions cannot justify inaction on the part
of religious educators in the areas of evangelization
and initiation. Fear may not mislead the religious
educator into the paralysis of merely "playing it
safe" and staying only within the stages of information or pre-evangelization.

Hundreds of priests, sisters and laity have gone
to TEC as team members, but have come home as
candidates. A bonus blessing from the exercise
has come from the clergy, religious and laity who
have come to understand and accept "renewal"
through insights given by candidates at TEC. It is
said of Simeon that the old man held the youth,
but the youth converted the old man. Our youth
may well lead us to the horizon of the twenty-
first century.

(This chapter based on original by Fr. Matthew
Fedewa.)

# 3
# Selecting
# the
# Team

A TEC team consists of a Lay Director, an Assistant Lay Director, Spiritual Directors, Adult Laymen, and Teen Laymen.

## LAY DIRECTOR

The Lay Director is selected by the TEC Council and should be a man or woman who is not only familiar with the TEC program, but has served on one or more TEC weekend teams. The Lay Director should be chosen six to eight weeks before the weekend to give him or her sufficient time to choose a team and plan for team meetings.

## SPIRITUAL DIRECTOR

In addition to the director(s) of the program, the Lay Director should engage three or four priests to be on the team. A Protestant minister is also a desirable addition since on most weekends a few of the candidates will be Protestants. If possible, try to obtain one priest with TEC experience and one who may, in the future, be in a position to recruit candidates for other TECs.

## ASSISTANT LAY DIRECTOR

One lay person selected for the team will serve as Assistant Lay Director. He or she should be someone the Lay Director understands and who understands the Director so that the two can work together closely, complement each other, and still make their own unique contributions. During the weekend the Assistant should be a close advisor and sounding board for the Director. Thus, the Assistant can help prevent the Director from becoming isolated or set apart from the action of the weekend.

The Assistant can also do many minor tasks on the weekend, thus freeing the Lay Director for his primary tasks. In essence, the Assistant should be someone who has already been a Lay Director or who appears capable of becoming one someday. Moreover, the Assistant should be prepared to take over the TEC if necessary.

## ADULT LAYMEN

At least four talks are given by adult laymen and probably six tables must be staffed. Thus, besides the Assistant Director, probably five other laymen have to be recruited. One layman will give part of the talk entitled "The Universal Call to Holiness," which part is referred to as "The Marriage Talk." The layman's spouse will share the presentation. Thus, in picking the team adult members, try to keep in mind that one of the members should have spouse who would be willing and able to share in this talk. Among the adults chosen for the team, there should be a male or female religious so as to be able to partake of the talk on the "Universal Call to Holiness," speaking specifically on religious life.

Seminarians may also serve on the team, but their level of training—high school, college, theology—will determine their role as an adult or teen team member.

Try to have a mixture of "veterans" and "rookies." The experienced TEC team member can be called upon for the more difficult talks (such as the "Christian Life" talk) while the new team member will provide a source of possible future talent for other TEC teams. Try to have a balance of various ages represented. The last talk by a layman ("Christianity in Action") is often best given by a college-age person.

The couple giving the Marriage Talk ("Universal Call to Holiness") on the other hand should, if possible, have been married for several years. Try to have a balance of "introvert" and "extrovert" personalities. Try to get people from as many different towns and cities as possible. Try to get as many races, cultural backgrounds, educational levels as possible represented.

27

The above suggestions on selecting the adult laymen can be summed up as follows: try to make the selection with a view towards having as many different types of people as possible. Of course, all of the above suggestions can never be realized in practice, but are, nevertheless, goals the Lay Director should work toward.

## TEEN LAYMEN

The teenagers on the team fulfill a vital and important role and without them TEC would not be what it is. Two of them give "witness talks" (so-called). Another serves as Music Director. In selecting the teen speakers, it is best to get young people who want to give a talk and have, through TEC, had a change in their life style. It is often helpful if they have just recently (within six months) made their own TEC. The Music Director should be capable of playing the guitar, sing fairly well, and able to lead a group in song.

With all the above suggestions, selecting a team may well seem like an impossible task. Well, in fact, Christ is the one really doing all the work. Just trust in His help and the Spirit will guide you. The TEC Council will be a big help in suggesting names of possible team members. People met on previous TECs are another source of help. Personal friends are also a big help but do not overload the team with close friends if possible as this may prevent the distribution of types suggested earlier.

# 4
# Role of
# Team
# Members

## THE LAY DIRECTOR

The Lay Director is responsible for the selection of the team and for the management of the TEC weekend. It is through the Director that the members of the team will come together in Christ. It is in the person of the Director that this particular TEC weekend will be focused and identified.

The Director should have experienced one or more TEC weekends. Experience in TEC is a prerequisite for selection as Director. It would be a good idea if the person selected reviewed the article "Teens Encounter Christ" by Fr. Matthew Fedewa reprinted in this manual. One of his first acts as Lay Director will be to explain TEC to the team, and he should therefore have "what TEC is" clear in his mind before that time.

The TEC team is truly a representation of the Church, the Body of Christ, the People of God. As

St. Paul describes it, each team member has a role to *fulfill* (not to *play*) and no one is superior to any other. The Director does not, for example, have to give himself in the unique way of the person who gives a talk. He does not necessarily have to impart theological insights in the way the Spiritual Directors do. He does not even have to spend hours each day of the weekend washing dishes in the kitchen.

What the Director does have to do is to select and form the team in consultation with the Spiritual Director and the TEC Council. This formation takes place at the meetings preceding the weekend. During the weekend he is responsible for the logistics of introducing speakers, deciding on variations in the schedule, and in general being sensitive to what is going on and thus being prepared to act accordingly. This role is, in a sense, a lonely one as he sits by himself in the conference room wondering how the table discussion is going.

Due to the nature of his role, the Director will tend to spend a little time with a lot of people rather than a lot of time with a few people. Some Directors will perhaps experience one or another member of the team or a candidate deeply. It depends on how the Lord uses the Director on a TEC weekend. The Director must make this clear to himself and to the team so that they will understand what is happening.

An experienced Lay Director, Dan Perry exhorts:

The Director should not interject his personality into things excessively. This is not to say, however, that you should stifle any urge you might have to comment, from time to time, on the talks, secretary's reports, and the general progress of the weekend. In other words—be yourself, don't try to assume the manner of some other Director you have observed. There is no mold for Directors any more than there is for people. Remember, you wouldn't have been selected unless it was apparent that you possessed the qualities required. Finally, the Director must be a man or woman of prayer who realizes his or her ultimate dependence on Jesus for guidance to do the job effectively.

## THE ASSISTANT DIRECTOR

The Assistant Director should be a person who can take over for the Lay Director at any time—prior to TEC or during the weekend itself. The Assistant Director should be involved in all of the planning with the Lay Director and Spiritual Director. The Assistant Director's role is truly one of service.

Some of the suggested jobs the Assistant can adequately perform during the weekend are:

A. Be a "materials person" i.e., checking out the supplies for the weekend (New Testaments, paper, pencils, pens, magic markers, poster paper, crosses, bread and wine and vessels for Mass, stoles for Baptism, etc.). The Assistant Director should supply each table and pass out materials as needed. He/she can prepare the chapel for each function as it arises.

B. Be a "Palanca person." Please see special roles below.

C. Be the Master of Ceremony for the Hootenanny. Since the Assistant Director is part of the TEC weekend, he knows the flavor of that particular

31

TEC. He can easily introduce the team and candidates as well as the speaker for the "Peace Talk."

## THE SPIRITUAL DIRECTOR

This role can be fulfilled by a priest, a Christian minister, a deacon, and at times, a religious brother or sister. The Spiritual Director is ordinarily a priest.

The greatest contribution the Spiritual Director can make is his presence as the person he is and the priest he is. He should be a clear witness to the Holy Spirit and to the gifts God has given him. He most particularly should be ready to render service in love to teens and team.

As Spiritual Director, a priest will be asked to:

A. Give talks drawing on theology and including the human aspect.

B. Lead liturgical and paraliturgical services.

C. Celebrate the sacrament of penance.

D. Provide counselling, if asked.

E. Join in table action after he has given his talk and become known to the candidates. Then he can really be accepted by the candidates as a person and not as an authority figure. The adult at the table can decide best when the time is ripe for the Spiritual Director to join in. Some Lay Directors prefer to have the Spiritual Director at the table from the beginning. They feel it is too difficult for the Spiritual Director to be accepted as a table member in the middle of the weekend. This movement to table is an option opened to the Spiritual Director at the discretion of the Lay Director.

## THE TEAM MEMBER

Each team member has to be available to the candidates, be a witness of faith, and help form a small Christian community. Although all are there to help and to give of themselves, team members find that they receive far more than they can ever give.

Each team member has the following responsibilities:

A. To be alert and sensitive to the general tone of the group. If, for example, candidates are restless, suggest to the Lay Director the need for a change of activity.

B. To try to get to know each one of the group assigned to a particular table. Be very conscious of the uniqueness and great potential power lying deep inside each person.

C. To take advantage of breaks and meals and free time to get to know as many of the candidates as possible. Being available is very important. By mixing with the candidates the preliminary ground-work for counselling is often accomplished.

D. To refuse to be the discussion leader. If the group looks to the team member for pat answers, he should throw the questions back at them.

E. To listen, and to take mental notes of reactions—observe on Saturday. The candidates will be confused and will have many questions. They may get off the track in discussions. Let them. As TEC unfolds they will give insights and understanding. Try to draw out their individual goodness and beauty.

F. To take the lead a bit more on Sunday.

G. To help guide the progress of discussion on Monday, making sure there are no misunderstandings.

H. To be alert at all times; to be a good listener; to be approachable and help the candidates clarify their personal objectives.

I. To report all problems to the Lay Director. Any corrections or discipline will be administered by the Director. Sometimes allowing candidates the freedom to make mistakes can have great impact.

J. To watch for small groups—those who are close friends at home. Join them.

K. To carefully observe candidates assigned to his table, especially the leaders. To help the leader do his or her job.

L. To keep candidates moving during the time for discussion, poster making, summaries, etc. If discussion is going well, play it by ear and continue. If summaries are given, make sure they are a group consensus and all take some part. Try to have the discussion on talks relating to their own lives or interpretation, not just a feedback.

M. To try to build the idea of a small community

at the table. Stress table support (for instance: at summaries, poster, etc.).

N. To take notes and participate in everything. To set the example. To take his turn giving summary or explaining the poster, but only enough to encourage the candidates that he is with them all the way.


Following the Piety talk on Sunday morning, team members are free to suggest that tables make a Chapel visit. Play this by ear. Sometimes following an involved discussion at table, this visit can be an important part of really getting to know one another. Try to avoid being in Chapel with other tables. Check with the Lay Director or other team members. Be certain to let the Lay Director know, so that he will be aware of a table's whereabouts.

We are not deliberately trying to wear out the candidates by the long hours, but experience shows that they will not retire before midnight, or even afterwards, especially when away from home. We recommend that you use every subtle means to suggest and urge them to get sleep. But remember that *any force* will only call forth rebellion, so be careful to preserve the element of freedom of choice.

Refrain from judging and analyzing during the weekend. Try to develop and transmit an attitude of faith, trust, and love. Be sure to attend each team meeting at the end of the day. The directors need this communication and opportunity to go over the next day's events and plans. This is also

*God reveals himself to the candidate in Christ and there is no substitute for this personal experience. The greatest good we can do for anyone is not to give him of our wealth but to show him his own.*

the time to bring up any problems and questions.

Some team members give talks. Each of these talks has a theme and certain points that must be covered. The method used is not lecture, moralizing, theologizing, talking how it should be, etc. The method is to emphasize the witness aspect, i.e., "This is how I came to my present feelings about it." It is usually quite effective to use personal experience relevant to the topic. Each talk should include a "personal introduction phase" so that the candidates will get to know the speaker personally and thus be more favorably disposed to receive what he or she is trying to get across.

Note: the phrase "medium is the message" really applies—just getting up in front of the assembled TEC and giving the talk is in itself the major portion of the message (witnessing).

Adult team members not giving talks—particularly if it is their first TEC—sometimes get the impression that they will be free-riders and not really make a contribution to the weekend. It should be noted that everyone will have the opportunity to talk to the group (if so inclined) during the weekend. In any event, the work at the tables and during off-hours is at least as essential as the talks.

Teen team members should *not* compare their TEC with this one. Teen members are a vital part of the team. They can provide a bridge between the candidates and the rest of the team. Their reaction will often reflect how the candidates will react.

To summarize the role of a team member: sensitivity, respect, humility, honesty, openness.

A religious should be a witness to his/her life and assume the same responsibilities as the other team members.

## PERSON WHO DISTRIBUTES PALANCA

This job can be done by the Assistant Director or any team member. But the Assistant Director is suggested because he is not responsible for candidates at table. The palanca person should have a complete list of team and candidates. Palanca should also be kept in a place where it cannot be seen by candidates. (See Chapter X, Palanca.)

The palanca person:

A. Should be certain there is palanca (two or three per candidate is great) for each candidate and team member for distribution on Saturday night.

B. Can give each team member a piece of palanca about 15 minutes before the person gives a talk.

C. Should not hand out very fancy palanca on Saturday night, unless necessary.

D. Should be certain there is some palanca addressed to the community to be read on Saturday night.

E. Should distribute palanca for the rest of the weekend in consultation with the Lay Director.

F. Should be sure there is a large container at the Hootenanny to collect all palanca so as not to lose any in the excitement of the Hootenanny.

## M. C. FOR HOOTENANNY

The basic task of the M. C. is to introduce the particular TEC to all present at the Hootenanny. The M. C. should make a complete list of all—team and candidates. The M. C. should also introduce the speaker for the "Peace Talk." The M. C. should keep the Hootenanny moving. A suggested form is:

A. Thirty minutes for music, songs, singing, dancing, greeting.

B. Twenty-thirty minutes—introduce TEC.

C. Thirty minutes—Peace Talk.

D. Ten minutes—final songs.

## BACK-UP CREW

This has also been referred to as "Kitchen Palanca." Some former TECers are usually needed to set up, serve, and clean tables for meals. They may also be needed to wash dishes. Other chores or odd jobs may arise that can be handled by the back-up crew.

If a person knows a candidate very well, it would be better for the candidate that this person does not serve on back-up. Candidates would tend to confide in this friend rather than build friendships with other candidates or team members.

## THE MUSIC DIRECTOR

Music is very important on the TEC weekend. It is part of the liturgical events. It is used between talks and at other times. It helps develop bonds of unity. The Music Director—a former TECer—leads the group in song. Songs chosen should fit the theme of the day and the mood of the moment. For example, it is not usually appropriate to sing "To Be Alive" on Saturday evening when many are experiencing for the first time the suffering and dying of the Paschal Mystery.

The Music Director should have a song ready each time so as not to waste time deciding "What shall we sing?"

A list of songs should be prepared by the Music Director before the weekend. Songs chosen for the liturgies on Sunday and Monday should fit the preference of the group. The Music Director can discern this by Sunday.

The Music Director should not play during the Hootenanny. Once this event begins, the Music Director should put the guitar aside and rest. The Music Director needs his energy and talent for the rest of the weekend.

# 5
# Team
# Meetings

Team meetings provide the opportunity for team members to get to know one another better and begin to form community among themselves.

Before discussing the individual meetings, a word first about attendance and frequency. When the Lay Director is selecting the team, each person should be told of the number of meetings and asked whether or not he is able to attend. If community is to be formed, presence is necessary. Adults who are new to the TEC program can learn much about the weekend from those who have already had the experience.

Going into the weekend "cold" or without instruction beforehand can be detrimental to the person functioning as a team member rather than as a candidate. If one who is asked to be on the team wants to serve but will miss the majority of team meetings, then it is better to ask the person to wait until he is able to attend all the team meetings.

At least three meetings are suggested before the

weekend. As many as five can be held, depending on the amount of work to be done. A very effective variation on the regular team meeting is to have an overnight team meeting. This gives the team more time together and more work can be accomplished in this extended time period.

A team meeting is held on Friday evening before the weekend starts. Moreover, there is a team meeting on Saturday and Sunday evenings, after the day's activities are completed.

Within a week to ten days after TEC, the team should meet for an evaluation of the weekend. This facilitates follow-up on candidates and produces learning for future weekends. A thanksgiving liturgy should be celebrated, if possible, at this team evaluation.

## FIRST TEAM MEETING

This meeting should be held five or six weeks before the TEC weekend at a location as central as possible to the various team members. It may be a good idea to mail out a reminder of the time and place with a set of directions or a map to each team member a few days before.

Try to obtain a room with a table all can gather around. Provide coffee and light refreshments. Have name tags for everyone.

The following is a suggested outline:

A. The Lay Director introduces himself and then requests each team member to introduce himself (name, town and parish, work or school, married, number of children, previous TECs, etc.).

B. State that the purpose of the meeting is to describe the TEC program in general and the weekend in particular and begin preparation for the TEC No.——weekend. "As we prepare through our meetings for TEC No.——, the bonds of community among us will grow. Like the weekend itself, we are right now beginning an encounter—a pilgrimage."

C. Bible Service:

1. Song.
2. Scripture reading.
3. Reflection/comment on the reading especially as it pertains to the task now beginning.
4. Our Father—all join hands as a sign of unity.

D. Content and Method of TEC (Refer to Fr. Fedewa's article). TEC means Teens Encounter Christ. Meditate for a moment on the meaning of those words. A real encounter—a personal experience—an experience in the development of a Christian Community. CCD, religion classes, and home training have told us that we should love one another, but we are often afraid to be open—to take the first step.

On TEC, trust is developed, personal encounter with others develops. The candidates see and experience that a group of 20 to 30 people can come to love one another. They *see* Christian Community (it's no longer just theory). When they leave TEC, they take with them—as a minimum —an experience they will never forget. For some, their lives are redirected on a new course (metanoia) toward God. TEC involves all the senses, the whole person, not just talk and reflection (intellectualizing).

E. Origin of TEC. See opening paragraph, Chapter II.

F. Elements used: Catechesis, Liturgy, Doctrine and (most important perhaps) Witness. To show how these elements are used, a summary of the TEC weekend—how it is laid out—how it unfolds— can be given. The theme of TEC is spelled out:

Saturday:   To *Die* in Christ
Sunday:   To *Rise* in Christ
Monday:   To *Go* in Christ

The object is to take the candidate through the "Pre-Evangelization" and "Evangelization" stages of spiritual development, but in general, not on to the "Catechesis" stage. (Again see Fr. Fedewa's article, section II.) The team and candidates are seated around five or six tables in the conference room.

1. A series of talks and meditations are given by Spiritual Directors, Adult team members and Teen team members. Frequently the talks by the teens are the most effective. After each talk the idea is repeated through a discussion period led by one of the candidates and sometimes via posters. A summary of the table discussion and an explanation of any poster is made by a representative of each table to conclude the exercise. Each talk builds on the previous ones.

2. The liturgical services seem to develop natural-

ly out of the circumstances of the times as true expressions of Christ in the community.

3. The Bible (Scripture) plays a vital role. Most talks are keyed to a passage from Scripture which is read to introduce the talk at first by a team member, but as the weekend progresses, by the candidates.

4. Music is very important on the TEC weekend. It is part of the liturgical events. It's used between talks and at other times to also develop bonds of unity.

5. *Palanca.* For further details, see Chapters IV and X. *Palanca* is a Spanish word meaning "lever." The idea is that just as with a see-saw (a lever), one person pushes down and the other one goes up. So when one person does a little spiritual dying, his pushing down spiritually lifts someone up spiritually (one dies so that someone else might rise).

*Palanca* usually takes the form of letters written to those making the TEC by people on the outside; friends, relatives, former TEC-ers. In the letters there might be a message of support; perhaps a penitential action will be mentioned. The whole idea of doing something for someone else becomes a "My Palanca for You" kind of thing.

6. Other elements of TEC:

   a) Freedom to accept or reject Christ ( a loving invitation is offered).

   b) Informal dress—to emphasize that we are all people, to de-emphasize our particular roles as priests, teachers, students, workers, professional people, housewives, etc.

c) Table arrangement—seats are assigned so that friends will not be together.

G. Explain roles. See Chapter IV.

H. At this point it would be good to ask for questions and have any others present, familiar with TEC, add their comments. This may well bring out the truth that "All TECs are different" since the former TECers will probably have quite different experiences to draw on. This discussion will hopefully develop into a general sharing of opinions on TEC, the Church, teenagers, adults, etc.

I. Coffee break.

J. Assignment of the talks. These assignments should be made before this team meeting by the Lay Director in consultation with the Assistant Director and a Spiritual Director who has had previous TEC experience. As the talks are assigned, give the speaker a copy of the TEC Manual, commenting on the talk outline and its place in the Progression. (See Chapter IX, Progression of Talks—Chart.) These outlines generally make the points to be covered in that particular talk. The examples used in making these points, however, are only models. It would be better to draw on your own experiences.

K. Final announcements:

1. Time and place of all team meetings. Stress importance of *everyone* attending *all* the

meetings. Assign a date to each speaker to give presentation at one of the team meetings. It would be beneficial, but not necessary, if the presentation can be made in the order which they occur on the weekend.

2. Content of next meeting—to begin going over the talks by the teen and adult laymen.

3. Applications and sponsor forms for candidates —make available to all team members.

4. Help arrange transportation for next meeting (sharing of rides, etc.).

## SECOND TEAM MEETING

The same arrangements should be made for all meetings with respect to room, table, nametags, coffee, etc.

A. Introductions—for those not previously present.

B. Review the first meeting and cover the following points. At this meeting it is important to be conscious of those who might not have been present at the first meeting. This would dictate the extent and depth of the necessary review. It is a good idea to try to draw out some of the impressions of the newcomers (either during the meeting or privately) in order that any wrong notions may be dispelled.

Make frequent and emphatic reference to the initially passive role of the team members at the tables during the weekend, especially the adults. Insofar as possible, try to give practical

*Music is very important on TEC weekends. It is part of the liturgical events, is used between talks and, through songs chosen to fit the theme of the day and the mood of the moment, it helps develop bonds of unity.*

discussion guides for the tables (other experienced team members can help). Stress the need for complete dedication by everyone on the team. All should be aware that the weekend is basically for the candidates and that the team is there to give of themselves. State that the main purpose of this meeting is to go over the talks.

C. Bible service (see above under first meeting for details of the Bible service).

D. Go over talks. The talks by those who have never given a TEC talk or meditation before should definitely be covered. However, as a model for others, you might ask an experienced "talk-giver" to go first. Make sure you elicit a response from the teenagers present as to their reactions to the talks—they will be a very good barometer as to how the talk will be received.

Comments by the Spiritual Directors and experienced TECers will also be helpful. It is necessary that the essentials of the talk be clear in everyone's mind. Because of the rather difficult nature of some of the talks, do not insist on every detail. Do not ask for complete talks to be written out. An outline of the talk, however, might be valuable in the future for other TECs.

E. Take a break in mid-evening and, as before, resume with a song.

F. End the meeting with any appropriate announcements.

## THIRD TEAM MEETING

Make the same physical arrangements as before. This may be the last meeting before the TEC weekend begins. By now everyone will be aware of what TEC is all about, at least to the extent of having developed a feeling for TEC. It is vital that everyone on the team should make his feelings known, especially if they are negative. This openness among the team will go a long way towards making the weekend a success. As Lay Director, try to develop this openness during the meeting tonight, if it has not yet come about.

A. It might be appropriate to begin by having a Spiritual Director, offer a spontaneous prayer and then reflect on the team's progress to date.

B. Go over the remainder of the talks. You may have to be flexible about this. For instance, a talk by an inexperienced person may need a second review. On the other hand, a talk by an experienced person (especially if you know that person's capabilities) may be skipped altogether.

C. Break.

D. Liturgy (suggested scripture: LK 24:13-35).

E. Announcements. Make sure everyone knows where the TEC center is located and the time of the Friday night meeting. Go over "what to bring" in the line of clothes, towels, etc.

# FRIDAY NIGHT TEAM MEETING

The TEC weekend begins on Friday night for the team. It is also, in a sense, the fourth team meeting. While the Lay Director and Assistant Director do Items A and B below, the rest of the team can be doing Item C.

A. Sorting applications. The Lay Director and his Assistant arrange the candidates' applications in five or six groups (one group for each table). Six tables is the normal TEC complement but if there are fewer than 30 candidates it is probably better to go with five tables.

   When arranging the candidates' applications, strive to keep people who know each other from sitting at the same table. This includes team members at the tables as well as candidates.

B. Team assignment. Ideally, there should be one adult layman and one teen team member at each table. When making table assignments try to balance personalities and TEC experience.

   The Music Director does not have to sit at a table (and probably should not) unless there is a shortage of team members. If the Music Director does sit at a table, it should be as a third team member since his primary function frequently keeps him away from the table.

C. Housekeeping Chores.

   1. Setting up the tables—arrange the tables, chairs and lectern.

   2. Name and address cards—team members can

fill out theirs now. Candidates can fill out theirs when they register on Saturday. Time can be saved at registration if a team member prints the names and addresses the night before from the application forms. This insures a clear form and decreases errors when the address list is compiled.

3. Name tags—a name tag for each candidate and team member.

4. Signs for counselling and/or confession rooms with names of Spiritual Directors on them.

5. Remove all posters, banners, etc. from the TEC conference room which are left over from previous TECs. One simple banner or poster stressing the TEC theme should be behind the lectern. A few others can decorate the room.

6. TEC prayer cards—these cards will be given to everyone at the end of the weekend on Monday afternoon. They all have to be signed by the Lay Director and a Spiritual Director. It might be a good idea to start signing them Friday night since time for this chore will be hard to come by during the weekend.

D. Team meeting.

1. Announce the table assignments for the team members and hand over the candidates' applications.

2. Table seating plans and teen table leader selection. The team leaders at the table take the candidate applications and make up a seating plan. In the process, they must select,

from the information on the applications, one candidate to be "table leader." This table leader, not the team members, will be responsible for leading the discussion at the table. In selecting a table leader an alternate should always be chosen in the event the original selection does not show or obviously seems to be the wrong choice when first met.

Using a "clock face" the table leader sits at the "12 o'clock" position facing the lectern. The adult at the table sits at "6 o'clock" with his or her back to the lectern. (The other team members can be at "3 o'clock" and "9 o'clock".) It is also worth noting that the candidate next to the table leader (at 1 o'clock) will be secretary for the table after the first talk and therefore will be the first candidate to come to the lectern to make a report.

Two seating plans should be made up— —one for the adult at the table, the other for the Lay Director. On the Director's seating plan, the team members might write a brief comment beside the name of each candidate, i.e., something unique about the candidate taken from his or her application.

For your own convenience, it might be helpful to have a list of candidates and team members with town and school, for each table rather than the clock-face seating plan. This list can then also be used by the Master of Ceremonies when he introduces the team and candidates during the Hootenanny.

Make sure all the applications are returned

to the Lay Director. None should be left around.

3. Review the role of the team as you did at the first meeting, especially for the benefit of those who missed that meeting.

4. Assignment of Scripture Readers for the Saturday talks. Each reading can be introduced by a short explanation or ended with reflection on the reading. Readers can at first be a team member, but later on, candidates may be asked to do this task.

5. Chapel Palanca—during each meditation, some other team member is in the chapel praying for the success of that talk. No one should do Chapel Palanca if he or she is to give a talk and has not given it yet. It is important to know what is said so that, if necessary, succeeding talks can be modified accordingly. For Saturday, volunteers for Chapel Palanca are needed for the following talks:

Ideals and Maturity
Paschal Mystery
Penance
Prodigal Son
Metanoia

After the talk, the speaker goes to the chapel to greet the person doing the Palanca. Important: the speaker remains away from the conference room until after the discussion period.

6. Bell Ringer—pick someone to ring the bell

which calls everyone to the conference room (in the morning and after meals and breaks). Try to get someone with an outgoing personality. Perhaps an adult not giving a talk. Do not give him or her the bell just yet.

E. Liturgy—a team liturgy can be celebrated at the end of Friday night's activity, or alternately, first thing on Saturday.

F. Odds and Ends—once the weekend begins the Lay Director will be too busy to think about the following so make sure they are all taken care of before it is too late.

1. Have the Spiritual Directors agree who will lead each liturgical service and have them go over the details of these services. The one who gives the *Penance* talk usually leads the Service of Ashes. The one who does the *Sign* talk usually leads the Sunday Liturgy.

2. Is the Sunday Evening Hootenanny all set?

3. The film or filmstrip used during the weekend—is it all set? Some one to set it up and to run the projector?

4. Ask someone such as an adult not giving a talk to take charge of registration Saturday morning. Get a list of candidates and give it to this person.

5. Make up a master list of candidates by table and/or alphabetically for use by the Lay Director.

6. Check what time group pictures will be taken.

7. Check if there is enough palanca for each candidate.

8. If small dormitories are used, appoint a team member to make a master plan of where all the candidates will be sleeping. Also, check that the facilities are ready.

9. Have part of the team prepare the chapel with banners, posters, etc. if necessary.

## SATURDAY NIGHT TEAM MEETINGS

Two very important meetings are held each night after the formal program ends.

A. Teen table leaders meeting with Lay Director and Assistant Director. Each table leader is asked to review his table as to how it reacted to the talks and any problems the table leader may be having (with his role or with others at the table). The table leaders can be advised that during Sunday they can relax a little as they become more and more free to join in the discussion themselves.

B. Team Meeting.

1. Each table is reviewed by the team members from that table. The Lay Director is here attempting to get an idea of what is happening at the tables since he is removed from them by the nature of his role.

2. Brief reminder that "Saturday we died, Sunday we rise."

3. Assignment of Scripture readers and chapel

palanca for Sunday for:
   God Is a Community of Love
   Christian Life (Piety)
   People of God
   Sign

## SUNDAY NIGHT TEAM MEETINGS

The format of these two meetings is the same as on Saturday night.

A. Teen Table Leader meeting with the Lay Director and Assistant Director.

   1. Review each table.

   2. Advise table leaders that their function can be dropped tomorrow (if they have not already done this) since everyone is, by now joining in the discussion.

B. Team Meeting.

   1. Review each table.

   2. Reminder "Saturday we died, today we rose, tomorrow we go forth."

   3. Assignment of Scripture readers and chapel palanca for Monday for:
      Universal Call to Holiness
      Church in the World
      Christianity in Action

   4. How to wake up if bells are missing? Traditionally, the team awakens the candidates by forming a marching band and parading through the dormitory with all manner of music and noise making devices!

On TEC, trust and personal encounter with others develop. The candidates become aware that a group of 20 to 30 people can come together to form Christian Community in fact, not just in theory.

# 6
# Candidates
# and
# Sponsors

TEC was originally drawn up for the high school senior. And in many programs, TEC still has the senior as the main focus. In different parts of the country, circumstances changed this focus somewhat. So it has become necessary to speak about the age of the candidate.

In the Archdiocese of New York, for example, the TEC Council has decided to work within the 17-to-23-year age span. Age 17 is used as a base because it is the average age of the senior in high school. Some high school seniors are younger than 17—and although younger candidates have made TEC, it would be advisable for them to wait, if possible.

The reason for this is that on the average, the older candidate seems to be more serious about his/her intentions and, consequently, takes the weekend more seriously. This also lessens frivolity and disciplinary problems. In line with this last point, it is not desirable that the Lay Director or any other team member become a "parent away from home." This vitiates the whole thrust of the TEC experience.

Age 23 has been established as ceiling age because many college students and working people within the college age span have applied to make a TEC. Rather than turn them away, the program has decided to accept older candidates. Their contribution to the program is unique and balancing.

The candidate is asked to fill out an application form (see below) and to write a personal letter to accompany the form. Both of these are important. An application form gives the team basic facts about the candidate. A personal letter about and by the candidate helps put bare facts into perspective and gives a clear picture of the person of the candidate. These two items (together with the sponsor sheet) help the team determine possible table leaders and separate candidates from the same place, school, parish, etc.

## SPONSORSHIP

If a person is interested in making a TEC, then it is necessary that the prospective candidate be sponsored. This means that a "sponsor sheet" must be filled out and mailed to the Applications Committee under separate cover (see below). Sponsorship entails this and more.

Who can fill out the sponsor sheet? Any former TECer or team member should do this. Only if this is not possible, should a parent, teacher, priest, or friend do so.

A person who acts as sponsor for a candidate has the responsibility to:

A. Provide a ride to the TEC Center if the candidate cannot do so.

B. Be sure the candidate has palanca for Saturday night. This means that palanca must be in before TEC begins or be brought to the TEC Center on Saturday morning.

C. Explain palanca to the candidate's parents, if possible and ask that they send some to TEC.

D. Be at the Hootenanny.

E. Prepare, invite and bring the candidate's parents to the Hootenanny. It is not desirable that close friends of the candidate, who are prospective candidate themselves, be brought to the Hootenanny.

F. Provide a ride back home for the candidate if necessary.

G. Speak with the candidate after he returns home on Monday or bring the candidate to a "debriefing" if one is held in his locality.

## TEENS ENCOUNTER CHRIST

### SAMPLE APPLICATION

*TEC DATES*

TEC     1—Boys—Sept. 11-12-13
TEC     2—Girls—Oct. 9-10-11
TEC     3—Boys—Nov. 13-14-15
TEC     4—Girls—Dec. 11-12-13

Today's Date ——————— TEC Date Preferred ————

Name ————————————————————— ——————
         (Last)          (First)         (Initial)

Address ——————————————————— ——————
      (Street)        (City-State)       (Zip)

Phone ———— Date of Birth ———— Sex M —— F ——

Parent's First Names ——————————————————

School presently attending ——————— Grade ————
        or
Full-time employment ——————————————————--

Parish ——————————— Location ————

Sponsor for TEC ——————————————————

Religious background: Catholic ————————
           Christian ———— (Please specify) ————

Interests: List school activities, sports, clubs, organizations in which you participate.

————————————————————————————— ——

—————————————————————————————————

————————————————————————————— ——

## SAMPLE APPLICATION

Do you play the guitar?                        Yes—— No——

Have you had any training in art?              Yes—— No——

Have you had any experience in drama?          Yes—— No——

  If yes, in what capacity? ————————————————————————

What kind of vacation (or after-school) jobs have you had?

—————————————————————————————————————————————————————

—————————————————————————————————————————————————————

—————————————————————————————————————————————————————

*Please Note*: 1. If you own or play a guitar, please bring it along.
2. Bring recreation clothes.
3. Bring one set of dress clothes.
4. Bring your personal toiletries.
5. Please leave your books, homework assignments, and radios *at home*.
6. In a short letter to accompany this application, please tell us about yourself covering such items as:

  a. Why I am a Christian.
  b. What I plan to do after graduation.
  c. What I consider the principal problems facing young people.
  d. What particular worries do I face today.
  e. Please include anything else you wish to note about yourself.

This letter MUST accompany this application. We will attempt to make groupings on a basis of needs and interests.

I understand that an offering of ———————— will cover the cost of the weekend. Enclosed please find ———————— partial payment.

                    Candidate's Signature ————————

Send your application, letter and money to:
                    TEC

# SAMPLE TEC CANDIDATE SPONSOR SHEET

Whoever sponsors or refers a candidate to the TEC program MUST complete this form and mail it to:

TEC

This form *must not* be given to the candidate.

Candidate's Name (Please print) ————————————

Please *circle* the appropriate adjectives or substitute your own and/or add comments as desired or necessary.

| EXERCISE OF LEADERSHIP | very little | below average | average |
| above average | | very much |

**EXERCISE OF LEADERSHIP**   very little   below average   average   above average   very much

**AREAS OF LEADERSHIP**   athletic   student government   academic   social   apostolic service

**MATURITY**   very immature   immature   average   above average   very mature

**PSYCHOLOGICAL ADJUSTMENT**   poorly adjusted   below average   average   above average   very well

Add comments particularly in regard to any personality problems this student may have.

————————————————————————————

————————————————————————————

**ABILITY TO RELATE TO OTHER STUDENTS**   poor   below average   average   above average   very good

**ABILITY TO RELATE TO ADULTS**   poor   below average   average   above average   very good

HOW WOULD YOU RATE THIS STUDENT AS A TABLE DISCUSSION LEADER?

not recommended poor average above average strongly recommended

HOW DOES THIS STUDENT RELATE TO THE INSTITUTIONAL CHURCH?

highly antagonistic   mildly antagonistic   indifferent/apathetic   rather positive and well-disposed   highly enthusiastic

**WHAT IS THIS STUDENT'S ATTITUDE TOWARD EUCHARISTIC CELEBRATION?**

antagonistic    indifferent/apathetic    rather positive and well-disenthusiastic                                                                         posed

FAMILY    sound/firm        broken marriage        deceased mother
                    deceased    father      only child      parental interest
                    wealth      poverty      apostolic
Obvious Tensions? Why?

**ON REVERSE SIDE, ADD ANY COMMENTS WHICH MIGHT HELP THE TEC TEAM MEMBERS UNDERSTAND AND DEAL SYMPATHETICALLY WITH THIS STUDENT.**

Sponsored by (Name) ————————————————————

Relation to student ——————————————————————

# TEENS ENCOUNTER CHRIST

(Sample letter sent to candidate after application is accepted)

You have been accepted to participate in TEC     —to be held
on ————————. Welcome to Teens Encounter Christ. TEC
takes place on Saturday, Sunday and Monday.

## WHEN AND WHERE...

Registration is between 10:00 a.m. and 11:00 a.m. Saturday morning. Please be at ———— by 10:30 a.m. on
Saturday. The exercise will end about 5:00 p.m. on Monday.
No one should come later or leave earlier. You would not
be able to understand the exercise if you did.

The weekends are held at ————————————
————————————————. (See enclosed map.)

## WHAT SHOULD YOU BRING...

Slacks or bermudas for recreation. Comfortable, casual
clothes for the majority of the time. Dress clothes for the
Liturgy. Toiletries. Materials for two overnights. ————
supplies sheets, blankets and pillow cases. Musical instruments—hootenanny style! DO NOT bring school books, school
work, or radios.

We should have on hand your ———— deposit with
your application. The balance of ———— is due upon
registration

Looking forward to meeting you.
Peace!

P.S. Please let us know as soon as possible if you will not be
able to come on the weekend.

# TEENS ENCOUNTER CHRIST

(Sample letter sent to candidate's parents upon arrival of candidate on Saturday morning)

Dear Parent:

Your son/daughter has come to TEC (Teens Encounter Christ) at ——————— for a weekend. As his/her parent, we are sure you are interested in the weekend.

TEC is a living experience, a unique experience. There are opportunities for private discussions with priests, brothers, sisters, and competent laity. Most important, TEC can be best described as naturalness under the guidance of adult Christian leadership.

The weekend is lived with comparative strangers from many different situations and backgrounds. Usually the group consists of approximately thirty young students, plus the "team" of adults which includes clergy, lay persons, and those who live or are preparing for full-time religious life. The team of adults is comprised of screened, competent and generous people representing all walks of life: mothers, fathers, educators, professional and non-professional people.

The format of the schedule is a series of talks by clergy and laity and some former TEC students. The talks which present the basic themes of Christian life and its application to daily living are then followed by table discussions and written summaries.

To sum up, TEC is a weekend of PEOPLE TO PEOPLE, living together, thinking together, listening together, praying together—sharing new concepts and attitudes. There is much more to TEC than this letter could possibly convey. There are new friendships born, new avenues of charity explored, a new consciousness of other persons and a new appreciation for the reality of Christ's love.

It is here that we would bring your attention to the fact that your son/daughter will be somewhat different when he/she comes home on Monday evening. Since the whole experience of the weekend is very REAL, he/she needs your understanding. He/she, hopefully, will want to share his/her new insights, his/her new self. Help him/her with your understanding and love.

Sincerely yours,

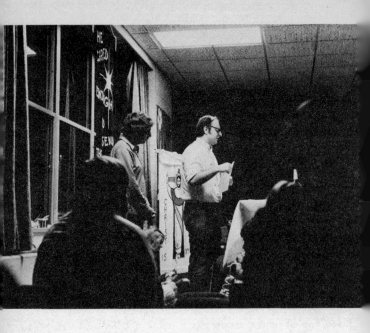

*There are many talks and each talk has a theme covering certain points. The method used is not lecturing, moralizing, sermonizing or theologizing but witnessing: "This is how I present my personal feelings about it."*

# 7
# Summary
# TEC
# Schedule

## A. SATURDAY

THEME:

"Unless the grain of wheat falls to the earth and dies ... "
(Jn 12:24)

"Through baptism into His death we were buried with him ... " (Rom 6:4)

| | |
|---|---|
| 10:30 | 1. Arrival, Registration |
| 11:00 | 2. Introduction |
| | 3. ORIENTATION TALK (regulations) |
| | 4. Table naming |
| 12:30 | 5. Lunch |
| 1:15 | 6. IDEALS AND MATURITY Talk |
| 2:30 | 7. Introduction and Enthronement of the Bible |
| 3:00 | 8. Break |

| | |
|---|---|
| 3:45 | 9. PASCHAL MYSTERY Talk |
| 4:45 | 10. PENANCE Talk |
| 5:30 | 11. Supper |
| 6:15 | 12. Meditation, PRODIGAL SON |
| | 13. Movie |
| | 14. Service of Ashes |
| 7:15 | 15. Scripture Reading at Tables |
| 7:45 | 16. METANOIA Talk |
| 9:00 | 17. Palanca |
| | 18. Quiet time for confession or conversation |
| 10:00 | 19. PASCHAL VIGIL Talk and Service |
| | 20. Announcements |

# B.  SUNDAY

## THEME:

"If it dies it produces much fruit." (Jn 12:24)

"So that just as Christ was raised from the dead by the glory of the Father, we too might live a new life." (Rom 6:4)

| | |
|---|---|
| 7:45 | 1. Rise |
| 8:15 | 2. Meditation, RISEN CHRIST |
| 8:30 | 3. Breakfast |

| 9:15 | 4. GOD IS A COMMUNITY OF LOVE Talk |
|---|---|
| 10:15 | 5. Short break |
| 10:30 | 6. CHRISTIAN LIFE—PIETY Talk |
| 12:30 | 7. Lunch and Break |
| 1:15 | 8. PEOPLE OF GOD Talk |
| 2:15 | 9. SIGN Talk |
| 3:30 | 10. Break |
| 4:30 | 11. Liturgy |
| 5:30 | 12. Supper |
| 6:30 | 13. Hootenanny (PEACE Talk) |
| 8:30 | 14. Skits |
| 9:30 | 15. General sharing time |
| 11:00 | 16. Night prayer |
| | 17. Announcements |

# C. MONDAY

THEME:

"As the Father has sent me, so I send you." (Jn 20:21)
"You are to be my witnesses . . . to the ends of the earth."
(Acts 1:8)

| 7:45 | 1. Rise |
|---|---|

8:15   2. Meditation, CONFIDENCE IN CHRIST

8:30   3. Breakfast

9:15   4. UNIVERSAL CALL TO HOLINESS
      a) MARRIED LIFE Talk
      b) RELIGIOUS LIFE Talk
      c) SINGLE LIFE Talk

10:30   5. Break

10:45   6. CHURCH IN THE WORLD Talk

12:00   7. Lunch

1:15   8. CHRISTIANITY IN ACTION Talk

2:30   9. Break for packing and cleaning up

3:00   10. BEYOND TEC Talk

3:30   11. Liturgy

5:00   12. Presentation of crosses

     13. Confirmation service

# 8
# Detailed
# TEC
# Schedule

## A. SATURDAY

THEME:

> "Unless the grain of wheat falls to the earth and dies ..."
> (Jn 12:24)
>
> "Through baptism into His death we were buried with Him ... " (Rom 6:4)

### 1. *ARRIVAL—REGISTRATION*

a) Two tables at front door, name tags for candidates on table, extra blank name tags (candidates may prefer nicknames), list of candidates with amount paid so far on table.

b) As each candidate arrives, team greets them, takes bag or suitcase.

c) They receive name tag—pay balance owed—fill out name and address card.

d) Escorted to TEC area: shown dorm, conference room, etc.

e) Guitarist should be playing guitar in TEC room.

## 2. INTRODUCTIONS

a) Have everyone stand away from the tables around the room.

b) Introduce self (name, town or city, married? number of children, work previous TECs?).

c) Introduce Spiritual Directors (each gives details as above).

d) Introduction of others and assignment of seat. A permanent place for the weekend. As you introduce yourself, come forward and give name, town or city, school or work, and your plans for next year, and why did you come to TEC.

e) Introduce back-up crew and other teen team members if they are not seated at tables.

f) Announce who the teen table leaders are (the first one seated at each table). State their function of leading the discussion and mention that you want to see them briefly right after this session.

g) Anecdote or joke to relax the atmosphere (optional) or singing.

# 3. *ORIENTATION TALK (REGULATIONS)*

a) A minimum of rules—a spirit of freedom for the good of all.

b) Candy, soft drinks, cigarettes are on the honor system. On leaving during the week-end—if you do, we must assume you've left for good and therefore we will notify your home. If you decide to leave, please see me or one of the Spiritual Directors first.

c) Drugs—including grass, alcohol and the hard stuff—two reasons why we can't have this around. First: Be fair to yourself—I hope you'll have a good experience here this weekend. If so, you'll want to be able to say that, what happened was *real,* not influenced by stimulants, depressants, in other words "Let's get high on people." Second: Danger to TEC and the TEC Center. If the authorities found out that anything like drugs was being used, it could destroy TEC here. If you did bring anything with you, please turn it in to myself or the Spiritual Directors. They will be returned, no questions asked when you leave (if you still want them).

d) Notebooks and the secretary—Assistant Director passes out pencils and notebooks, one for each person and one for the table. Explain how each talk will be followed by a discussion and how the table secretary will report to the group on this discussion. Table secretary is a rotating function. Put names on notebooks.

e) Bell ringer—introduce and hand him or her the bell. When the bell rings, come to the conference room. Please respond quickly. We can't start until everyone is present.

f) Describe TEC area: conference room, dorm, cafeteria for meals.

g) Final comments: Relax—try to live each moment. Don't waste time wondering what comes next. DON'T ANTICIPATE. Even I don't know what is ahead for sure. Get involved (P A R T I C I P A T E)—share—meet others—mix at meals and on breaks. Don't analyze—just take things as they come. When you leave, the people around you will seem a lot different than they do now.

h) Anecdote—Optional.

i) Single out teen table leaders and ask them to stay—rest go to lunch.

j) Meeting with teen table leaders—explain their function:

   —To lead the discussion after each talk.
   —Draw everyone into the discussion—keep it moving (except adult)—tone down anyone who tends to dominate.
   —Responsible for getting all members of the table assembled when the bell rings.


## 4. TABLE NAMING


Assistant Director passes out materials (card, magic markers). This is the first function we do together in our table groups. Examples of names "Sunshine," "Seekers," etc. First chance for teen table leader to lead by explaining the table name to all.

5. *LUNCH*

A group picture will be taken sometime Saturday, depending on the photographer's schedule.

6. *IDEALS AND MATURITY TALK—*
   *TEEN SPEAKER*

Give this speaker a good introduction as he or she has a tough job breaking the ice. Stress that the speaker is not a professional orator, but rather wants to share some ideas with the group. The content of the talk is on the idea of the maturing of the person and how the person's ideals change (mature) as he or she gets older and approaches adulthood.

Normal session schedule:
  a) Introduce speaker.
  b) Talk.
  c) Table discussion.
  d) Secretaries' reports.
  e) Posters.
  f) Description of posters.

### 7. *INTRODUCTION AND ENTHRONEMENT OF THE BIBLE—TEAM MEMBER*

a) This ceremony introduces the Bible to the candidates as a vital force and important resource on the weekend. The speaker should explain as much as possible about the Bible and how to use it (Chapters—Verses). The speaker should explain the presence of God-Christ in His Word.

b) A copy of the New Testament or the entire Bible is distributed to all.

c) Bible is enthroned in Chapel—and/or conference room.

d) *Optional*—proceed to Chapel. Enthrone Bible. Have candidates open the Scriptures and read passages.

e) Paschal candle can be lit at this time or during the paschal vigil service.

### 8. *BREAK*

### 9. *PASCHAL MYSTERY TALK—THE THEME OF TEC—SPIRITUAL DIRECTOR*

The content of this talk is that it is the keynote address for the weekend. It may not take hold with candidates when given, but later on in the weekend they will come to appreciate it more as they experience their own Paschal Mystery.

Normal session schedule:

a) Reading pertinent to Paschal Mystery.
b) Introduce speaker for talk.
c) Paschal Mystery Talk.
d) Table discussion.
e) Secretaries' reports.

10. *PENANCE TALK—SPIRITUAL DIRECTOR (FAMILIAR WITH ADOLESCENT PSYCHOLOGY)*

This talk and the discussion after (Penance) may start before dinner and end after, or all may take place Saturday evening. It is more effective if given after supper. We have discovered that this discussion period becomes beneficial if tables center around problems they have with the Sacrament of Penance and the secretary presents these to the Spiritual Directors in the form of questions for response. The talk is on the idea of "metanoia" or turning towards God.

Normal session schedule:

a) Bible reading for Penance talk.
b) Introduce speaker.
c) Penance talk by speaker.
d) Table discussion.

11. *SUPPER*

## 12. *MEDITATION ON PRODIGAL SON—TEAM MEMBER*

This is a meditation based on the passage from Luke which is read as part of the talk. A suggested place for delivery is the Chapel.

Normal session schedule:

a) Introduce speaker.
b) The meditation.

## 13. *MOVIE*

A movie can be shown at this point. It changes the mode of presentation. It should relate to the theme of the evening—penance and metanoia. A suggested film is "The Stray." Feed-back and comments should be taken on the film.

## 14. *SERVICE OF ASHES (OPTIONAL)*

Will be lead by the Spiritual Director who gave the *Penance* talk. Make sure that the candidates are encouraged to partake of the Sacrament of Penance.

## 15. *SCRIPTURE READING AT TABLES (OPTIONAL)*

Each table is assigned a set of Bible readings. From one or all of them the table agrees on a "petition" or "prayer" to be delivered by the table secretary. This petition should express what the table as a group is repentant about as a result of reflecting on the Bible reading (s).

## 16. METANOIA TALK "CHANGE OF HEART"— TEEN SPEAKER

This talk sets the stage for the Baptismal service by describing what is meant by a change of heart, a metanoia, a turning towards God. This is a personal witness talk and need not be a very drastic metanoia to be effective.

Normal session schedule:

a) Introduce speaker.
b) The talk.

## 17. PALANCA

Letters, posters, banners, etc. sent into the TEC center by people working and praying for the success of the weekend are usually introduced sometime Saturday evening. This introduction could be based on what was said to the team at the first meeting. Alternately, a Lay Director, Assistant Director or Spiritual Director may introduce the concept of Palanca. Most of the Palanca will not arrive until Sunday evening and can be distributed then. Try to see that everyone, especially every candidate, gets some sort of Palanca. In introducing Palanca one might read a selected letter or two, particularly if one directed to the TEC is available. The distribution of the letters is best done during the breaks, so as not to distract the candidates.

## 18. QUIET TIME FOR CONFESSION OR CONVERSATION

In addition to the Sacrament of Penance, the Lay Director can encourage candidates to reflect and/or speak with team members during this time. Before quiet time begins, a small piece of paper can be handed to each person. A Spiritual Director asks that:

a) They write their sins down.
b) No one will see this paper.
c) It will be destroyed by them.

These papers can be burned either at the Service of Ashes or at the beginning of the Paschal Vigil Service. If the latter, then the Paschal candle can be lit from this fire. Symbolism: papers represent us—our sins. But despite our sins, we are God's creation and *goodness* or *light* (paschal candle) can be ours.

## 19. PASCHAL VIGIL TALK AND SERVICE—THE SERVICE OF LIGHT

The Spiritual Director will lead this service in the Chapel. Baptismal stoles are needed. The Paschal candle can be lit at this point and remains lit for the entire weekend.

## 20. ANNOUNCEMENTS

It is sometimes appropriate for the Lay Director to briefly summarize what has happened so far and perhaps bring things into perspective. In any event, at the end, announce:

a) Meeting with teen table leaders immediately (give location).

b) Meeting with team in a few minutes (give location).

c) Time for getting up Sunday morning— stress the responsibility of all to get a good night's sleep and not to disturb those who are already in bed. (Again, freedom.)

# B.   SUNDAY

THEME:

"If it dies it produces much fruit." (Jn 12:24)

"So that, just as Christ was raised from the dead by the glory of the Father, we too might live a new life." (Rom 6:4)

## 1. RISE

## 2. MEDITATION, RISEN CHRIST—TEAM MEMBER

This meditation is often presented before breakfast. Its object is to set the mood for the day—one of joy and celebration.

Normal session schedule:

a) Introduce speaker.
b) The meditation.

## 3. BREAKFAST

## 4. GOD IS A COMMUNITY OF LOVE TALK—SPIRITUAL DIRECTOR

God is usually quite a remote and abstract concept in the minds of young people. This talk brings God into focus as the Living Force within us.

Normal session schedule:

a) Bible reading.
b) Introduce speaker.
c) "God" talk by speaker.
d) Table discussion.
e) Secretaries' reports.
f) Posters.
g) Explanation of posters.

## 5. BREAK

## 6. CHRISTIAN LIFE—PIETY TALK—ADULT LAYMAN

This is the first talk by an adult layman. It is a very important talk. In it the speaker first tells what Piety *is not* and then tells what Piety *is*. Usually the speaker ends this talk with an invitation to all join him in the Chapel for prayer. Make sure to discuss the logistics of this possible Chapel visit with the speaker before the talk. The decision to go to the Chapel cannot be made until the talk is over since the talk itself creates the mood for action. It is most important that the Chapel visit be spontaneous and natural and not at all forced.

Normal session schedule:

a) Bible reading.
b) Introduce speaker.
c) Piety talk by speaker.
d) Chapel visit.

## 7. LUNCH

## 8. PEOPLE OF GOD TALK—ADULT LAYMAN

This talk relates the Christian to the Christian community by stressing the role of the Christian in the Church. The talk comes at a time when it is difficult for those who were up late the night before to stay alert. Sometimes this talk sets the stage for a Confirmation Ceremony.

This is better deferred until Monday because Confirmation involves a commitment the candidates may well not be ready for on Sunday. Also, Confirmation is associated with the theme of Monday "go forth" or "Pentecost."

Normal session schedule:

a) Bible reading.
b) Introduce speaker.
c) "People of God" talk.
d) Table discussion.
e) Secretaries' reports.

9. *SIGN TALK AND THE CELEBRATION OF THE EUCHARIST—SPIRITUAL DIRECTOR*

In preparation for the most important sacramental sign, the Eucharist, this talk brings out the idea of signs and symbols and their meaning as we travel the road of life or experience this TEC weekend together. The introduction could mention the signs already encountered (Penance, Baptism). There is no discussion after this talk.

Normal session schedule:

a) Bible reading.
b) Introduce speaker.
c) "Sign" talk by speaker.

10. *BREAK TO DRESS FOR LITURGY*

The idea of dressing in your "Sunday best"

seems to be lost somewhat. But this heightens the idea of the Eucharistic Celebration that we build up to all day, as something very special.

## 11. *LITURGY*

Often the high point of the day.

## 12. *SUPPER*

After Mass, all go to the dining area for the Sunday supper. In order to get ready for the Hootenanny WITHOUT THE CANDIDATES KNOWING IT, the Music Director can begin a Song Fest right in the dining area towards the end of the meal. In this way, the candidates will not wander off and learn of the impending Hootenanny.

## 13. *HOOTENANNY—PEACE TALK*

The Hootenanny will be led by a Master of Ceremonies, the Assistant Director of the TEC. The Peace Talk is given by a member of the TEC community.

## 14. *SKITS*

After the Hootenanny, the candidates will be experiencing many things. One suggested way to

bring all of these experiences into focus—
especially joy—is to have each of the tables
(including the directors) put on a skit. Allow
for preparation (about 15 minutes). It is interesting at this point to note how the tables
are becoming more cohesive and harmonious
by each person's contribution to the skit.

## 15. GENERAL SHARING TIME

Candidates are allowed to express themselves.

## 16. NIGHT PRAYERS

## 17. ANNOUNCEMENTS

a) Meeting with teen table leaders immediately.
b) Meeting with team in a few minutes.
c) Time for getting up Monday—again stress
that it is a good idea to get some rest and to
be fair to those who are trying to sleep.

# C.   MONDAY

## THEME:

"As the Father has sent me so I send you." (Jn 20:21)
"You are to be my witnesses . . . to the ends of the earth."
(Acts 1:8)

Monday's theme is "to go forth with Christ." The Monday experience is pentecostal. The schedule presented here is only one example of how this day might be experienced. Many variations are possible.

*Note*: Make sure everything is set for the presentation of crosses, pictures and cards at the end of the TEC. The Lay Director has to sign all the TEC cards. Be sure everyone has a TEC card.

1. *RISE*

2. *MEDITATION, CONFIDENCE IN CHRIST— TEAM MEMBER*

   This meditation is often given before breakfast, although this may not be a practical arrangement on all TECs.

   Normal session schedule:
   a) Introduce speaker.
   b) The meditation.

3. *BREAKFAST*

4. *UNIVERSAL CALL TO HOLINESS*

   a) Married Life—Talk
   b) Single Life—Talk
   c) Religious Life—Talk

A married couple (team member and spouse), a team member who is single, and a religious give these talks. Each talk is followed by a question period.

5. *BREAK*

6. *CHURCH IN THE WORLD TALK—SPIRITUAL DIRECTOR*

Yesterday in the "People of God" talk we heard about what the Church is and how it is a community of people with a purpose. This talk gets into the area of how this Church/community "goes forth"—what the role of the People of God is in the world. By now the TEC will have advanced from table community to a definite group identity. For this reason, instead of table discussion, general discussion around the room is more appropriate.

Normal session schedule:

a) Bible reading.
b) Introduce speaker.
c) "Church in the World" talk by speaker.
d) General discussion.

7. *LUNCH*

## 8. *CHRISTIANITY IN ACTION TALK—TEAM MEMBER*

It is now close to the end of the TEC weekend. The group has by now experienced what Christianity is. But, what about outside in "The world"? This talk begins the preparation for the return of the candidates to their everyday lives. It describes how a Christian acts in the world. This talk can be followed by a general discussion with other members of the team joining the speaker in an informal way. Alternately, the speaker may choose to begin preparations for the afternoon liturgy immediately by having each table make a collage.

Normal session schedule:

a) Bible reading.
b) Introduce speaker.
c) "Action" talk by speaker.
d) Possible general discussion.

## 9. *BREAK FOR PACKING AND CLEANING UP*

## 10. *BEYOND TEC—TEEN MEMBER*

This talk should be given by a TECer who can speak of the "do's and don't's" that give the candidates more help for their re-entry into the world. TEC follow-up programs are often mentioned.

## 11. *LITURGY*

In preparation for the Liturgy, each table can make a collage using clippings from old magazines. These collages should express the TEC experience of each table. At least a half to three-quarters of an hour will be required for this project. The collages can, during the Liturgy, be nailed to the large wooden cross as symbolic offertory gifts or as part of the penitential rite at the beginning of the Mass.

## 12. *PRESENTATION OF CROSSES*

Each candidate and team member is presented with a TEC cross. The Lay Director invests everyone saying: "NAME, Christ is counting on you!" Before the crosses are distributed, a team member can explain the symbolism seen in the cross—e.g., flat corpus, not protruding because Christ must come forth from you.

## 13. *CONFIRMATION SERVICE*

This, together with the presentation of crosses, is effectively done after Communion of the Mass. After each candidate has been invested with his cross, he can proceed to the Spiritual Directors for renewal of his Confirmation. Each candidate and team member is presented with an envelope containing names and addresses, and a TEC application form. A card, with the TEC prayer on it and signed by the Spiritual Director and Lay Director is also given to each. Envelopes should be distributed after Liturgy so as not to be a distraction to the candidates.

## TEC PRAYER CARD

### Life is a Pilgrimage...

To be on a Pilgrimage is to go through Christ to the Father/under the impulse of the Holy Spirit, with the help of Mary and all of the saints,/as you bring your brother along with you.

TEC _____    Date _____

_____    _____

Lay Director          Spiritual Director

# D. FINAL NOTES ON SCHEDULE

The TEC weekend for the candidates really begins after lunch on Saturday. For the Lay Director, a change in the "style" of his role also takes place at this time. Up until then, the Lay Director has been, more or less, the focus of the TEC, from the initial formation of the team, through team meetings and up to the orientation talk on Saturday morning. After this point, the weekend begins in earnest and what happens from here on definitely does not depend on any one person. The Lay Director's main function will consist in:

1. Adhering to the schedule or departing from it if the need arises.
2. Introducing the speakers.
3. Chairing the meetings at the end of the day with the team and with the teen table leaders.

One of the more difficult judgments to make is to cut off discussion at the tables. One clue (other than a need to cut it short due to lack of time) is when the Lay Director detects an increase in the "laughter level." It probably means the discussion is getting frivolous and it is probably best to stop. Some Lay Directors find it helpful to have an arrangement with one or more of the experienced adults at the tables so that by a look or a gesture they signal when their discussion is winding down.

The following is the "maximum" content of a session:

1. Bible reading with a short (one to five minutes) commentary.
2. Introduction of the talk (introduction of the speaker and the subject).
3. Talk (meditation) by the speaker.
4. Table discussion on the talk. Secretary takes notes on the discussion. Teen table leader leads the discussion.
5. Secretaries' reports to the group.

6. Poster made at each table expressing the table's reaction to the talk.

7. Poster described to the group by two members of table—for each table.

Frequently, there will not be time for the posters, although a poster should definitely be done after the "Ideals" talk and probably also once on Sunday morning.

*Caution*—do not let the candidates know a poster is to be done until after the secretaries report to the group. Otherwise, the candidates will worry about the posters to the detriment of the discussion.

One of the purposes of posters, as with table summaries, is to get the point of the preceding talk across to the group in a different way. Thus, if there are six tables and both summaries and posters are used, the point can be made 12 times.

The college, if used, is very time-consuming and is best deferred to Monday when the colleges can summarize the entire weekend and then be nailed to the Cross as part of the final liturgy.

Even the table discussion and summaries can be varied. After the Penance talk, the summaries are often replaced by a question and answer period.

Sometimes there is no table discussion after a talk. This is true for all the meditations and for the "Christian Life" talk if a Chapel visit follows directly after the talk.

When introducing the speakers, the Lay Director tries to tie the theme of the talk into what has already been said. After the talk, the Lay Director may also wish to make a brief comment on the talk.

An important function of the Lay Director in any of the group ceremonies such as the Baptismal and Penance Ceremonies is to preserve the freedom of each candidate not to participate in that service if he or she is so inclined. The logistics must therefore be such that there is no pressure to take part, and that anyone who chooses not to participate can do so without drawing attention to himself. It is vital that all the team members and the Spiritual Directors be made aware of this.

Some form of physical exercise is necessary, especially during the latter part of Saturday. This may be a game or just a walk outdoors for a few minutes.

# 9
# Progression
# of Talks
# Chart

| TITLE | TYPE | SPEAKER | SCRIPTURE | SCHEDULED |
|---|---|---|---|---|
| 1. Ideals of Manhood/ Womanhood | Talk | Teen | Mt 5:3-12 Phil 3:12-14 | Saturday 1:15 pm |
| 2. Bible Enthrone- ment | Short Explana- tion | Team Member | Lk 10:25-37 | Saturday 2:30 pm |
| 3. Paschal Mystery | Talk | Spiritual Director | Jn 12:23-26 1 Jn 3:14 Rom 6:3-11 8:1 | Saturday 3:45 pm |

| LENGTH IN MINUTES | PURPOSE | PROGRESSION |
|---|---|---|
| 20-30 | Talk should be an "ice breaker," whereby a person tells about his growing awareness of who he is becoming as a person and the helps and hindrances he has experienced. | As we mature we choose ideals we see in other people and model our lives after them. The ideals we choose can imprison us by making us selfish, and hinder our growth, or they can liberate us from selfishness and thereby aid our growth. Jesus is a person who has shown us ideals. |
| 10 | Talk should give basic description of Bible, including use of chapters and verses. It should include how God speaks to us in His word and should emphasize the presence of God in His Word. | In order to have ideals, we must experience them from persons. Jesus is seen as a person in the Word, and His presence and ideals are found therein. |
| 30 | Talk introduces theme of T E C weekend: through death to life in Christ. Real meaning of life is found in mystery of tensions in ourselves. It shows how Jesus faced these tensions which led to death and new life. We will plunge into mystery this weekend. | Jesus Christ came into the world where selfishness imprisoned man. He experienced tensions, but went through a process of liberation from this evil and reached new life. To follow Jesus, we are invited to go through this same process He did—His paschal mystery. |

| TITLE | TYPE | SPEAKER | SCRIPTURE | SCHEDULED |
|---|---|---|---|---|
| 4. Penance | Talk | Spiritual Director | Lk 22:33-34 54-62 Mt 9:11-13 | Saturday 4:45 pm |
| 5. Prodigal Son | Meditation | Team Member | Lk 15:11-32 | Saturday 6:15 pm |
| 6. Metanoia | Talk | Teen | Acts 9:1-18 | Saturday 7:45 pm |
| 7. Palanca | Short Explanation | Lay Director | 1 Cor 12: 12-31 | Saturday 9:00 pm |

| LENGTH IN MINUTES | PURPOSE | PROGRESSION |
|---|---|---|
| 30 | Talk should bring to maturity ideas of sin, metanoia, healing. Talk should show that as disciples we must face ourselves as we are—look at our weaknesses and bring these to the healing of the Sacrament of Penance. | In order to suffer and die with Jesus, we must be willing to transform our lives. Penance as a sacrament of transformation helps us in the healing process. Spiritual Director should not dwell on sin nor be legalistic. Tone should be gentle and healing. |
| 15 | Meditation should touch all three characters in the parable—the father who loves, the prodigal who changes his heart, the brother who has dificulty comprehending all. Talk should emphasize "celebration"—joy over one who returns. | An example from Scripture of one who changed his life from sin back to God. Parable brings out the difficulty involved in "turning around"; the father's attitude is complete acceptance in love and joy. |
| 20-30 | Talk is truly one of personal witness as to the change of heart in one's life in following Jesus. This is usually very ordinary and should be given simply. Candidates can relate to metanoia in every day living. | A person who has chosen Jesus as an ideal to follow can share how transformation - change of heart - metanoia has taken place. This talk shares who one was and who one is now - attempting to follow Jesus. |
| 10 | Brief explanation of what this Spanish word means—emphasizing the positive aspects of sacrifice. | Gives all an idea of those who are willing to suffer and die for the candidates and team, all done in and through Jesus Christ. |

| TITLE | TYPE | SPEAKER | SCRIPTURE | SCHEDULED |
|-------|------|---------|-----------|-----------|
| 8. Paschal Vigil Service Talk | Talk | Spiritual Director | Jn 1:1-14<br>Jn 8:12<br>Jn 3:5 | Saturday<br>10:00 pm |
| 9. Risen Christ | Meditation | Team Member | Mt 28:1-10<br>Mk 16:1-8<br>Lk 24:1-12<br>Jn 20:1-10 | Sunday<br>8:15 am |
| 10. God is a community of Love | Talk | Spiritual Director | 1 Jn 4:7-21<br>Rom 13:10<br>Jn 3:14-16<br>Eph 3:17 | Sunday<br>9:15 am |

| LENGTH IN MINUTES | PURPOSE | PROGRESSION |
|---|---|---|
| 15 | Talk shows that one begins his liberation from evil and fear when one is baptized and joins a community of believers who are trying to choose the God-life as the Good life. All are invited to personalize their choice at the Baptismal paraliturgy. This begins dying to self process. | After celebrating the sacrament of healing, metanoia is brought into ritual celebration in baptismal renewal. Baptism plunges us into the paschal mystery. We are experiencing transformation and desire the new life of resurrection. |
| 10 | To set the theme for the day: the risen Christ—living right in the body of this community—brings us joy, peace, love. | As people of new life—risen people—resurrected people, we have Jesus as our example to follow to the Father. |
| 30 | As God is a community of persons, sharing life and love, so should we be a community of life and love. We turn to the Father as children and to each other as members of His family. Man experiences God when he experiences love. | We are called to live new life in relation to God. We experience God's new life for us in the bosom of a loving community. We must live the law of love in community as Christians. |

| TITLE | TYPE | SPEAKER | SCRIPTURE | SCHEDULED |
|-------|------|---------|-----------|-----------|
| 11. Christian Life— Piety | Talk | Adult | 1 Cor 13: 1-13<br>Mt 7:15-22<br>Lk 11:1-13 | Sunday 10:30 am |
| 12. Church— People of God | Talk | Adult | 1 Cor 12: 12-31<br>Eph 4:4-6<br>Jn 13:35<br>Mt 5:48<br>Acts 2:45-47 | Sunday 1:15 pm |
| 13. Sign | Talk | Spiritual Director | Mt 26:26-27<br>Phil 2:5-10 | Sunday 2:15 pm |

| LENGTH IN MINUTES | PURPOSE | PROGRESSION |
|---|---|---|
| 20-30 | Christian life is Christ living in us. We must be witnesses to this life in our relationship with God and our neighbors. Our deeds show our love and our faith strengthens our deeds. Faith in love relationship is bolstered by prayer. | This talk continues the theme above by showing that a real personal relationship can be established between human and divine. This relationship—our Christian life—is built upon what we do (apostolate) and what we say (prayer). |
| 20-30 | God is a community. The Church is a community—the visible human expression of the divine community to the world. Speaker should show we are members of this community—the people of God. Analogies, e.g., puzzle, are helpful. | In living our Christian life, we are members of a body—Christ's body—the Church. As such, we are known as the People of God. |
| 30 | Talk shows how these relationships we have with God and each other are celebrated by means of an event sign called Eucharist. This event sign relives the suffering-dying process and celebrates the new life we have in Jesus. | As a people of God, we have our unity in the Eucharist - celebrating the Lord's presence in our midst in the sign of the bread and wine. |

| TITLE | TYPE | SPEAKER | SCRIPTURE | SCHEDULED |
|-------|------|---------|-----------|-----------|
| 14. Peace | Talk | Member of TEC Community | Jn Chap. 14 | Sunday 7:30 pm at Hootenanny |
| 15. Confidence in Christ | Meditation | Team Member | Mt 28:19 | Monday 8:15 am |
| 16. Universal Call to Holiness— Married Life | Talk | Adult and Spouse | Ecclus 26:1-4 16-21 1 Pet 3:1-9 Tobit 8:4-9 | Monday 9:15 am |

| LENGTH IN MINUTES | PURPOSE | PROGRESSION |
|---|---|---|
| 20-30 | Calls the TEC community to a reflection on the words of John's gospel concerning the peace of Christ. Should be a reflection from the speaker's viewpoint. | Hootenanny, from the name itself, is a song fest. Peace talk is given within a song context. A person sings the phrases from John's gospel and speaker reflects after each verse is sung. |
| 10 | Theme of Monday is to "go forth in Christ and proclaim His paschal mystery." We need confidence to do this. This meditation should instill this confidence. | In order to live a Christian life, we must be able to go forth in the Spirit with complete confidence. Be spontaneous and sensitive to all that has gone on before. |
| 30 | Every Christian has a call to holiness and there are various ways to live holy Christian lives. Talk establishes matrimony as a sacrament that two people continue to confer on each other. Union is likened to that of Christ with the Church. Each partner is both Christ and Church, saving and being saved by the spouse. | We are called to holiness in marriage. Difficulties as well as joys should be shared. Young and old married couples, childless or with many offspring, have effectively given this talk. |

| TITLE | TYPE | SPEAKER | SCRIPTURE | SCHEDULED |
|---|---|---|---|---|
| 17. Universal Call to Holiness— Religious Life | Talk | Religious Brother or Sister | Song of Songs 2:8-12 Jerm 1:4-8 Mk 10:28-30 | Monday 10:15 am |
| 18. Universal Call to Holiness— Single Life | Talk | Adult | Rom 1:4-8 | Monday 11:00 am |
| 19. Church in Modern World | Talk | Spiritual Director | Mt 5:13-16 10:16-21 32-39 Mt 13:33 | Monday 11:30 am |
| 20. Christianity in Action | Talk | Team Member | Mt 10:16 Jas 2:14-24 | Monday 1:15 pm |

| LENGTH IN MINUTES | PURPOSE | PROGRESSION |
|---|---|---|
| 20-30 | To present religious life as one avenue of living out the Christian call to holiness received at Baptism. It is important to present religious life in the total picture of Church and vocation in the broadest sense, and not as an isolated or elite call or higher state. | The talk uses personal examples and history to illustrate the reality and down to earthness of religious life. It views the vows and community life as means to make the basic elements of the Christian life so concrete and visible that they cannot be missed by the total Church community. |
| 20 | Talk should show how holiness is part of one's life as single person in society. | We are called to holiness in single life. If one has chosen this state, then an effective and healthy viewpoint for sharing is present. |
| 20-30 | To see that the Church is not an island unto itself but rather a sign in God's kingdom. We are to be persons—Christians of "yeast" in the "dough" of the world. | We are asked to be God's people of joy seeking holiness right in the world where we are. The speaker is encouraged to try to tie in as much of what has already been said up to now. |
| 20-30 | Talk should acquaint all with existing apostolic action and get them to know how and what they can do. | We are told in detail how we can give deeds to our faith, what we, who call ourselves Christians, should be doing in our daily lives. |

| TITLE | TYPE | SPEAKER | SCRIPTURE | SCHEDULED |
|-------|------|---------|-----------|-----------|
| 21. Beyond TEC | Talk | Teen | 1 Pet 3:8-17 | Monday 3:00 pm |

| LENGTH IN MINUTES | PURPOSE | PROGRESSION |
|---|---|---|
| 15 | Talk should bring all back to reality and help guide all to their future actions. This talk should make all realize the need for caution in speaking about TEC to others. Helps bring the candidates back to the same world he left. Should list future TEC events. | Finally, we are to be gentle in spreading the message of Jesus to others. Our hearts may be burning with love, but we will not have to shout about this. It will be seen by all. |

We are all aware of the hunger among our young people for something to rescue them from the stifling mediocrity and meaninglessness of contemporary life. TEC speaks clearly and uncompromisingly to their deepest needs.

# 10
# Talks
# and
# Meditations

In this section note that the talks and meditations are in outline form. It was felt that talks printed in their entirety soon would be dated. However, there are some exceptions.

We have included sample talks for "Ideals and Maturity," "Metanoia," and "Single Life." Only the sample "Metanoia" talk was written from the outline which precedes it. We included a sample for "Ideals" because this is the first talk of the weekend and should be well done. We feel a sample of this talk will be a source of encouragement.

We included a sample of the "Metanoia" talk because this is a very personal talk and also to emphasize the fact that the metanoia does *not* have to be a very drastic change in one's life. An ordinary change of heart is seen as possible for many. We included a sample of the "Single Life" talk because this talk is not given frequently—and a good sample talk is necessary.

All the meditations except one are in outline form. We printed the "Risen Christ" as an example of a completed form of meditation.

These talks and meditations are meant to be a guide and not something to adhere to slavishly. They are helps, and the Lay Director, former TECers and team members should be able to shed further light on these examples from their own experiences.

Finally, we encourage all to examine carefully the chart on the Progression of Talks so as to have an idea of how and where one's talk or meditation fits into the plan of the entire weekend.

# SATURDAY:

*IDEALS AND MATURITY—OUTLINE*

A. Man/Woman

1. What is man/woman? What elements make up a man?

2. Are you a man/woman? If so, what has established this for you? (Give examples)

3. Society's definition of a man/woman.

   a) He/she must perform certain acts.

b) He/she must behave in a certain manner.

c) He/she must achieve a certain status.

4. Use examples of how society tries to establish its own definition of man/woman.

B. Distinction between IDEALS and GOALS

1. Definition of an ideal.

a) Something that remains constant.

b) Something that you yourself must realize.

c) Are ideals ever reached?

2. Definition of a goal.

a) Something that depends upon the ideal you have set for yourself.

b) Goals change as you mature.

—As a youngster
—As an adolescent
—As a teenager
—As a mature adult

3. Exemplify how your goals should work towards your ideal.

C. Your ideal should be to become a mature adult man/woman.

1. This ideal is obtained by several means.

a) Man/woman conforming to society's standards.

b) Conforming to your own standards. Do you follow the crowd to become a man/woman or do you follow your own set of values?

2. The key to maturity is honesty.

a) You must be honest with yourself before you can be honest with others.

b) You must be willing to stick up for your beliefs and face the wonder of seeing yourself.

3. Exemplify all the points about ideals and goals with your own story of how you formed your ideals and how you are maturing into an adult.

D. Briefly mention how Christ should naturally fit into the lives of everyone in the room. Your concept of Christ must mature as you do.

E. Conclusion.

I have an ideal and have set goals to reach that ideal. Everyone in this room has an ideal whether or not he realizes it. Have you set your course to obtain that ideal or are you just following the crowd? How far are you willing to commit yourself to fulfilling the purpose of your life?

## IDEALS AND MATURITY—SAMPLE TALK

Philippians 3:12-14

It is not that I have reached it yet, or have already finished my course; but I am racing to grasp the prize if possible, since I have been grasped by Christ (Jesus). Brothers, I do not think of myself as having reached the finish line. I give no thought to what lies behind but push on to what is ahead. My entire attention is on the finish line as I run toward the prize to which God calls me—life on high in Christ Jesus.

It's a strange thing, but when I sat down to write this talk, I did something that I had never done before, and it struck me as being strange that this is the first time I had ever done it.

I knew that I wanted very much to do this right so I wanted to create the proper atmosphere in which to work. So I took from my rather messy dresser-top a candle—one that I had received last Christmas as a gift from a friend but I never lit it because I knew that that would disfigure it. I didn't want to ruin it, its beauty, or the memory of the thought behind it because this candle was in the shape of the circle with the arrow—the biological symbol for man.

As it turned out, I wasn't able to get through the first paragraph very well because that candle wouldn't give enough light. So I decided I should get another candle. Well, the only other one I had was in the shape of a baby chick—another gift— also beautiful and important—but it seemed that to include this in my talk would sort of "blow the mood" because physically it did not match up to the other more impressive candle.

Well, this seems a very silly way to begin a talk on ideals and maturity—because after all what do candles have to do with it. But after writing the first few paragraphs and thinking about all the implications made within them, I realized that my talk was practically all planned out.

Maturity is something that you can't really put your finger on, like the flame of the candle, but if it's there you will always know it and if it's not, you will know that too. Maturity is not something to be judged physically. The "man" candle was the more physically mature but the smaller "chicken" candle was the one that seemed to be putting up the bigger fight to give me light.

Also, it is evident that the small candle is going to burn out quicker, but in doing so, it will have achieved something worthwhile—it will have achieved its purpose. Once the larger candle gets past the arrow segment, the wick can only go either right or left. And once it goes down, it can't go back up and therefore it will always leave behind half of itself—unused and unus*able*.

The flame of either candle can flicker or dwindle which signifies periods of uncertainty or periods of falling out—such circumstances are characteristic of both man and candle. It's also possible for the flame to be hidden within the physical structure of the candle, as is the case with the "man" candle. This candle has the same potential for light as the smaller candle but it has not let itself be seen.

Finally, there is the possibility of the draft or the breeze, which puts the candle out. The candle's only ideal was to be lit and to burn and to serve as light for man. (Blow out). So now the candle has burned out and we must enter into a world without it, no longer depending on it to draw conclusions. Having already seen the light, we must be ready to consider man—you and me and them.

Well, most of the talks I've heard or heard of concerning ideals and maturity and attitudes and manhood, when given from a personal point of view, have been given by members of a class of people known as older adults. Belonging to this class, they have most likely become married or not, according to their express choice, have a job they've chosen, may have had several jobs prior to their story, etc.

What I mean by all of this is that they have a particular chapter or chapters of their life finished and ready to relate, whereby they can instruct or demonstrate. To the contrary, I am in the middle of an episode in my life with no more sureness to relate than that which I have. Sure I can tell you about the time I was ten and wanted a certain small job very badly and how at fourteen I wanted a raise in that job. But that is behind me. I'm different and what I seek should and *must* be different.

Now I have no specific job in mind as I did then because now, along with thinking about that job, I must think about what I want to do for a major part of the rest of my life, what *I* can do for *it*, what *it* can do for *me*; if *I* can do *it*, if *it* can be done. My maturity has not reached that level of ripeness yet. But I feel that I cannot be too upset because if, under pressure, I choose something that I know I can do, just so I can hurry up and do it, I may someday suffer for it.

So, in speaking about ideals now, the most I have to offer are feelings that are identifiable, in most cases, characteristic of the majority, but in all cases, me, a person with no "chapter" completed but very much interested in writing the book which I want to be good enough to be published—at least one copy that I may keep in my bookcase in a place of satisfaction and fulfillment.

My ideal, (it is only one, but it probably has a million parts), is to put myself up to others to SHARE and BE SHARED. Within this I see a situa-

tion of LOVING and BEING LOVED, UNDER-
STANDING and BEING UNDERSTOOD, HELP-
ING and BEING HELPED, CARING and BEING
CARED ABOUT. And, of course, there are hun-
dreds of other aspects of life that can be mentioned
here. But all of those things involve a TWO-WAY
RELATIONSHIP, a DO and a BE DONE UNTO.

That is the way I want my life to be. I see nothing wrong with taking. The proverb "To give is
better than to receive" is true but I feel that if you
can have both actions working together, you've
really got something. If, by taking something, I can
give someone the joy that they give me when *they*
take what I have to offer, I will do that.

Ideals are formed as something to strive for and
something that will give person satisfaction when
achieved. But in order to ever achieve results from
the process, something else is needed—a something
that makes the difference between a day-dream
and a true result. Sure it's fine for me to say "I'm
gonna share and be shared." But what does that
mean?

Does that mean that I want to wear a sign that
says "Hey everybody, here I am. Come to me. I'm
gonna share with you. You need a coat? Here, take
mine. I don't need it. If I give it to you that's
better."? No, I don't mean that at all. The reason
is because that is not me. I need to have the
maturity to realize that. That is, I must have the
ideal to be me and the maturity to make me be
something.

I have the ideal of being of value to others.
Along with that I must have also the maturity to

realize there are only certain ways to do so. For instance, I can't be an engineer *and* a social worker; nor can I be a priest or brother *and* be married. And going one step further, maybe I can't be any of these things, just as I can't be the totally self-giving person previously described.

But I can be me and I can make that person something valuable. If I frequently take an inventory of myself, reminding myself where I am, what I'm doing, and, most important why, and can act on the answers, then I'm achieving my ideals as far as they reach at this time.

At this time, I could probably be in one of the largest and best colleges in the state, but yet not be me, the person. But if that is going to ruin the only ideal I have and shut me off from others, I can't accept that now. That is, I think, what happens with too many people.

For instance, some of the best workers in big corporations are not happy because they did not foresee that somewhere along the line their values got clouded, and now they're doing something they have the talent and ability to do, but lack the real makeup to do it. They have turned away from the *me* part of themselves and have gotten it mixed up with something else and sooner or later they will have to come to grips with the problem.

If I can live without ever ignoring *me,* I'll always have the ability to do big things but they must not overshadow what I am, or else my ideals, which should be most important to me, are suppressed and it may take all the maturity in the world to bring them back.

Maturity and ideals, then, work together in making the complete person. I have the ideal of being the better me, the approachable me, the loving me, the caring me—but I must always question myself —do I have the maturity to be these things?—not just on Tuesdays, or days off, or days when I'm done with other things, or days when I've had enough sleep? My answer better be yes because today is none of those days but it's a day I want to be all of those things.

## BIBLE ENTHRONEMENT

A. The Bible a book.

1. The Bible as a book includes a variety of topics such as:
   a) War stories.
   b) Accounts of national history.
   c) Poems.
   d) Prayers.
   e) Narration of the life of a great person.
2. The Bible gives us a basis for our religious faith and reveals the meaning of life itself.

B. The Bible is not a single book but a collection of books divided into two sections.

1. The Old Testament tells of the history of the Hebrews from the very beginning of time. It sets the stage for one of the most dramatic events of our time.
   Examples:
   a) The first book—*Genesis*—tells of creation,

the flood and other events concerning man and his Creator.

b) The Prophets—the spokesmen for God. Mention and speak about some of the prophets.

c) Psalms—used as Hebrew hymnbook and contains their expression of worship.

d) Wisdom Literature—Books of Proverbs and Ecclesiastes for examples. These books deal with man as an individual, not with the Hebrew people alone. They deal with man and his relationship to other men and to God.

2. The New Testament tells how God, acting as Christ, effectively overcame sin and made His goodness known.

Examples:

a) Gospels—four accounts relating Jesus' life. Speak about Jesus being Messiah yet dying as an outcast.

b) Acts of the Apostles—having spoken about God the Father, and Jesus the Son, Acts treats of the Holy Spirit and His working in the Church.

c) Paul and his Epistles—in Paul's letters, God reveals his purpose for us—to create a community in which men can be themselves. Speak about this more fully.

C. Having mentioned the division of the Bible into the Old Testament and the New Testament and the further division of books, talk about using the Bible—chapters, verse, etc. Give an example.

D. God teaches us in the Bible about life and He also speaks to us about love. Opening the Bible to any page, the love of the Lord is truly apparent. He is present in His word. Talk about the Lord's presence in His word and how He speaks to us personally.

## THE PASCHAL MYSTERY

(An introduction to the Theology and Psychology of TEC). Note: As many concrete signs (images) as possible should be employed in order to explain more clearly this most fundamental mystery of Christianity.

A. Introduce and explain the death—resurrection mystery of Jesus and our participation within that mystery.

1. Baptism plunges us into the Paschal Mystery of Christ.

2. Paschal Mystery—Suffering—Death—New Life.

   Paschal Event

   Easter Event

3. Events in the last moments of Jesus' life.

4. Mystery—not something we do not understand, but something we grow more in every day.

5. We are baptized Christians—we are Easter people.

6. We must understand this Easter Event we live.

7. Understand meaning of death—life not ended, finished, but transformed—changed.

B. Change—may or may not result in growth.

  1. Examples of change:
    a) Physical world—ice to water to steam or decomposed leaves and debris to soil.
    b) Changes of our physical being—greying, aging or moving from one location to another.
    c) Changes in our personality—in our attitudes.

  2. Changes in the third category are the most crucial: they can be regressive or progressive.

    a) Regressive
      —More indifferent
      —More turned into ourselves
      —Use my neighbor
      —Degrade myself
      —Complacent with negative, stagnating ideas of Christ and the Church
         } DISHARMONY (man in conflict)

    b) Progressive
      —More loving and accepting of myself and others
      —More caring
      —More concern
      —More open-minded to learn
         } HARMONY (man at peace)

C. But if we want these good things to happen, we will have to struggle (sacrifice)—core of TEC. Jesus Christ had to suffer (the cross) in order to bring about something good. "We must die in order to live." He used the example of the grain of wheat to demonstrate His point: "Unless the grain of wheat falls to the earth and dies...." We will use a similar example—the seed (a seed of a plant or a bean.)

1. Example of the seed: all the nutriments for the future of this plant are contained within the seed. The potential is there. Everything inside is good, but sleeping. It needs to be planted in good soil, needs water and plenty of warmth. What happens? In the soil the seed dies, so that new life can spring from it. IT DIES SO THAT IT LIVES. IT IS NOT DESTROYED, BUT TRANSFORMED.

2. Application to ourselves:
   —There is good within ourselves, we are important.
   —Certainly we have failed, but we can, right here, right now, place ourselves in a new frame of mind.
   —We, like the seed before it buds forth, struggle—we are bored, anxious, uneasy with ourselves and others.

D. During the TEC, we will reintroduce ourselves in a new way to:
   Christ in Scripture.
   Christ in Sacraments.
   Christ in each other.

E. What will happen on TEC?
   1. Maybe we can open to new ideas—let the old, stagnant ones die.
   2. Maybe we can regain the art of listening to

God and to one another with the inner ear.

3. Maybe we can take off the mask.

4. Maybe we can accept and love ourselves a little more.

5. Maybe we can accept and love others a little more, no matter who they are—the unpopular people; the unfriendly people.

F. The challenge: Take the risk of the weekend. We have all searched for peace in so many different ways. Let's try Christ's way for once. Stay with it. Challenge yourself and your ideas of Christ. Don't keep running to your friends from your school or neighborhood. Open yourself up to meeting new people.


## PENANCE


A. Sin—mature our concept.

1. Inadequate ideas:

   a) Sin is a "blot on my soul"—immature.

   b) Sin is "breaking the laws of God"—too legalistic.

2. More adequate ideas:

   a) Refusal of a relationship of loving dependence on God.

   b) Failure to maintain a love relationship with—oneself
      —others
      —God

   N.B. This failure may be *slight*—e.g. harsh words with someone; *serious*—e.g. vicious argument; or lead to a *break*—e.g. I refuse to love you!

3. Sin considered in this way—a failure to maintain a love relationship—is more of an attitude—not a single action.

B. Metanoia

1. Change of heart must occur first.
2. Scripture exemplifies this:
   a) Jonah—City of Ninevah repents "When God saw their actions, how they turned from their evil way ...."
   b) John the Baptist preached repentance.
   c) Peter's denial and change of heart.

C. Penance

1. Sacrament—an encounter with Christ in a specific role or way.
2. Penance—encounter with the forgiving and healing Christ.
3. What does one share?
   a) Not a "grocery list"—immature.
   b) But refusals to grow in loving relationships with God, self, and others.
4. Why confess to a priest?
   a) Because he is a leader of the Christian community.
   b) As leader or representative of the Christian community, he accepts one's sorrow and he offers forgiveness and healing of Christ and of the Christian community.
   c) Our sins affect others (social aspect).
      —our immediate community—family, school, peers.

            —the Christian community.
            —therefore, to "confess" only to God
            ignores healing within the community.
  5. Sacrament of Penance is celebrated:
     a) Because of the joy of healing and forgiveness.
     b) Note the "celebration" upon return of the Prodigal Son.
  6. Healing (reconciliation).
     a) Perform one's "penance."
     b) Begins with the celebration of the sacrament.
     c) Must be completed in the community.

     E.G. Appendectomy—healing begins at the hospital with surgery; healing is completed at home with rest.

  7. Conclusion—James 5:16 "Hence, declare your sins to one another, and pray for one another, that you may find healing."


*THE PRODIGAL SON*


A. Point of the parable is the father.

  1. The conduct of the son was not unusual—we demand and then regret: that is all too familiar to all of us.

  2. We think that God would act like I would act if I were that father, but Christ teaches that He does not.

B. Story of the son could be mine or yours.

1. He "collected all his belongings and went off to a distant land." (Lk 15:13)

2. "He squandered his money on dissolute living." (Lk 15:13)

3. "Famine broke out . . . and he was in dire need." (Lk 15:14)

4. He was sent to "take care of the pigs." (Lk 15:15) the low life and wretchedness of his state. Jewish father ordinarily did not take back son who did a "gentile" thing, i.e., feed pigs.

C. A reaction sets in.

1. It is hard for him to take the first step.

2. What will friends, neighbors, and brothers say?

3. How will his father receive him?

4. But then we hear the finest words a man ever speaks: "I will break away and return to my father." (Lk 15:18)

D. How the father reacts.

1. "He was still a long way off, his father caught sight of him." (Lk 15:20)

2. His father "was deeply moved." (Lk 15:20)

3. "He ran out to meet him." (Lk 15:20) The old man begins to run.

4. He "threw his arms around his neck, and kissed him." (Lk 15:20)

5. "Let us eat and celebrate." (Lk 15:23)

E. Not a slave but a son.

1. Slaves went barefoot, and had only a loin cloth.
2. Sons had a robe, sandals, and a ring. The father gives these to the boy.

F. Human attitude to the forgiven sinner is portrayed by the older son.

1. He "grew angry at this and would not go in." (Lk 15:28)
2. "For years now I have slaved for you." (Lk 15:29)
3. "...this son of yours..." (Lk 15:30)—he would not call him his brother.

G. The arms of God are open to us this evening— they are the arms of Christ, as we will encounter Him in the Sacrament of Penance.


## METANOIA—OUTLINE


A. Introduction
1. Explanation of Metanoia (change of heart).
2. Definition—turning away from self. Everything does not revolve around myself.

B. My change and my relationships.

1. Myself—harmony within myself.
   a) To believe and be proud of it.
   b) Not to compromise my beliefs when it became easy for me to do so because of selfish wants.
2. Christ—harmony outside myself.

a) My past schooling.

   1) Christ is an authority—grammar school.

   2) A teacher telling me Christ can be related to, but not letting me do it for myself—high school.

b) After my change of heart.

   1) Christ as a one-one relationship (friendship).

3. Neighborhood.

a) Compassion instead of anger at the people who put me down for my race, or nationality.

b) Understanding of poverty rather than condemning people for not getting a job.

4. Family.

a) Not being different just to prove I am better than them.

b) Trying to avoid conflict by staying away from areas in which I disagreed with my parents, rather than staying away from my parents.

c) Trying to communicate with my parents rather than just acting out my role as son to them on the basis of need, i.e., "What's for dinner?" "Can I have some money?"

d) Emphasis on subtleness of change—not a dramatic one. Parents and I have not conquered the generation gap but we have a much better time around the house.

5. Friends.

a) Change in my desire for freedom, i.e., change from the chains of drinking every Friday night to prove I was free, to the freedom of not drinking when I don't want to. I would wait all week to go drinking on Friday night, and then find I wasted a whole week of school, so that I could be "free" on Friday night, and finding out that come Friday night, I really wasn't free.

b) Started relating to my friends about their joys and sorrows, i.e., someone's new girl friend, a sick parent, etc.

C. Conclusion.

1. Change from a taking on of responsibility— a getting into others and out of myself.

2. Freedom is the courage to believe or not to believe, to do something or not to do it. It takes this courage to break habits that bind us and then we are free.


## METANOIA—SAMPLE TALK


This is called the Metanoia talk and I bet the first question that comes to your mind is what is *Metanoia*? Well, the definition I was given is a change of heart or a change of attitude, but for myself I define it as *a turning away from self,* which means a realization that my problems, my likes, my dislikes and my joys are not the problems, likes, dislikes and joys of everyone in the whole world.

In other words, I learned that I was not the center of the universe, that everything did not revolve around myself. So when I say turning away from self I mean that I started rejoicing in the joys of others, crying in their sorrows, etc.

Well, there were a lot of people that I had to deal with and all different types. I started to become a different person, and it was funny to look at the people I work with in a more sensitive way than I ever did before. And then there were parents, friends and even myself. Well, the first person I had to deal with concerning this change was myself.

What this turning away from self created was a harmony within myself. I didn't feel like a phony as much as I had in the past. There now was more harmony between by practice and my preaching. I found a courage to believe, and to make known that belief and to take joy in it. There was a change in me in the way I thought of Christ.

I went through twelve years of Catholic school and in the first eight I was taught that Christ was an authority figure and then in my last four years I was taught that Christ could be related to, but that never got the point across because, a teacher, an authority figure in itself was telling me this; so no matter how I tried, I still saw Him as an authority figure.

But when I finished TEC and went through change of heart, I really started to see Him on a one-to-one basis and not the good-little-boy-praying-to-the-Almighty-Father that I was taught I was. This helped me to turn away from self because first, I learned it through a group of my peers and not by going home and studying my catechism, and secondly, because it put me in a one-to-one relationship with Christ, therefore giving me a new responsibility and a little less time to think of myself.

One example of this inner self-harmony that came about when I experienced metanoia, happened to me shortly afterward. You see, I hang out in the South Bronx, and according to your leading newspapers, this is supposed to be a really messed-up neighborhood. And when I had turned to the Lord, the change of heart that took place was one of understanding.

I began to understand the arrogance and the hatred that brewed in people who had ten or more brothers and sisters, who sat in a classroom with sixty other children, or those who had had their work incentive taken away by a very apathetic welfare system.

I really started to identify more and more as I went on, and some of the stuff that I was immune to before began to really touch and disgust me in a bad way. And when this hatred touched me, for instance, times when I was called "white boy" or any similar remark, I reacted with forgiveness and understanding, rather than with arrogance and hatred.

The next people that I had to deal with was my family, which is just my parents and my grandmother. You know we talk about relating and that we want to be relevant. Well there is a very weird feeling, when you notice yourself relating on an intimate basis with your parents. Yeah, my father with his crew cut and all, was telling me stuff that all my supposedly "relevant" friends would never think of in their whole lives.

When I was about fifteen I was starting to become a liberal and just like everyone else I was against a lot of the things the grown-ups were handing us, but it wasn't the beliefs in the legalization of marijuana, or the anti-war stand that made me feel the most like a liberal. It was getting in fights with my parents that made me feel it the most, because now I was thinking for myself, and of course my thoughts were right, and theirs were wrong. After all, all my friends agreed with me.

I used to feel so cool because here I was thinking for myself. Well I turned away from that. I found that I rarely wanted to get political with them any more and when I did, I found myself listening to them. I started to feel that I would rather talk to them and find out what they're like rather than to get in fights with them.

You know as far as parents are concerned I never could talk to them about relatives. I don't know how many of you can sympathize with this but I bet some of you don't know the names of all your aunts and uncles and to which one of your parents they are related. Well I actually found myself listening when my parents talked about Uncle Billy and Aunt Mildred. That's when I knew that something had changed in me, and it got me a little worried.

I'm only kidding, of course, but it is really weird for me to be getting into my parents' problems and noticing that they have troubles no different from regular people. I really love my parents now, but, of course, I still experience some difficulties talking to them. But I experience difficulties in talking to anyone every now and then, even with my girl friend or my best friends.

Before my turning away from myself, things were all right with my parents but we communicated only on basis of need: "Go to the store!" or "Can you lend me $5.00?" "What do want to eat?" or for nothing else to do. Like if I were sitting in my kitchen listening to the radio and my mother is sitting there and we haven't said anything to one another for the last ten minutes so my mother would say "Who is that singing?" I would say "So-and-so" and before I was finished my mother would have said "Oh" not really listening.

But now after my turning away from self, my mother knows everything there is to know about my favorite singers and I know everything there is to know about hers. See metanoia is no big dramatic change. Me and my parents aren't going to go out and conquer the world, but by communicating and sharing I have a more pleasant time when I am home. And that's what people are for—they are there for your joy—use them.

Anyway, getting back to metanoia, I also experienced a change of attitude, a turning away from self when it came to friends. One of the big things that I left, probably the biggest, was my desire for freedom. I often put up walls against what I knew was true, because I thought that turning away from myself would put me at the mercy of others and thereby take away my freedom. And I thought that if I followed Christ's teachings I could not be free.

You see, my friends, the group I hang around

with, we drink an awful lot every weekend. I would live for weekends, because then I thought that the unfreedom of school and work was off me, and now I could be free. But then I found that wow! You know school is pretty important and here I am hustling, without paying attention, through my school week so that I can go out with my friends come the weekend. I was not really free because, just as I had to go to school, I had to go drinking.

I said to myself, wow! You are really in a rut, because week after week I had wasted my whole time in school, so that I could be free on the weekend. And then I was slapped in the face with the fact that I had wasted the whole week and I wasn't free *not* to drink on the weekend.

Well the turning away from self came when I realized that I wanted to be with my friends on the weekend, but to rejoice in a story about someone's new girl friend or to participate in the sorrow of a sick parent, not to get myself drunk with them.

So now I found myself loving my friends more than I had before. I still drink with them, but instead of saying "I'm going to drink three bottles of wine because I'm free to do so" I now want to sit with a bottle for maybe four hours, with the same bottle, just sitting and talking.

Because now that I have turned away from self I would rather be listening to music with my parents than to be sleeping on the stoop after drinking three bottles of wine. Because when I'm talking with my mother I am participating with another human being. Whereas if I'm sleeping in the street, I'm only wrapped up in myself and I am not free because I'm tied up in myself.

So just as in my parent's case I'm not going to conquer the world, and I wasn't an alcoholic who has been cured or anything dramatic like that, but instead I just like to talk about trivial or tremendously important things with others, because that is how love grows.

In conclusion, I will say that my turning away from self came from a taking on of responsibility, by getting involved with others rather than going on about my own ways caring only about myself.

Concerning Christ I am happier now that I have gotten to know Him and when I hurt Him, I am glad to owe Him the responsibility and the love to say I'm sorry rather than hurting Him and saying "Who cares, I'm free to do what I want."

Concerning myself, I'm happy to say I wonder what Cathy or Rene are doing right now rather than thinking of how much money I need to buy a new stereo.

Concerning parents, I am happier to say "Hi, guess what happened at school today" rather than "Hi, what's to eat?"

Concerning friends, I am happier to say "Hey, did they fix your car?" or "Hey, is your father all right?" or something else about them rather than saying "Wow! this is my third bottle and I'm messed up."

The things like "How's your father" provoke a conversation to grow, which in turn helps love to grow.

The thing that I learned the most was that freedom comes from courage to believe or not to, to do something or not to, and what I gained most is courage.

I hope and pray that I and you may always have the courage to be free to do or not to do.

## PALANCA

Palanca is a Spanish word that means lever, crowbar, or a bar used for carrying a load. For example, if you were seeking a job where I work, and I spoke to my boss for you, that would be palanca.

Diagram of a simple lever using above example.

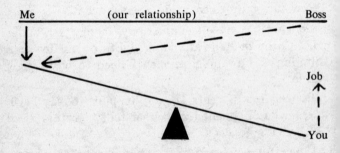

There are people out there who are speaking to the Lord, and are asking Him to intercede in our lives this very weekend—to help you develop a relationship with Him.

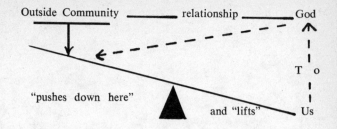

Outside Community ———— relationship ———— God

"pushes down here"

and "lifts"

To Us

Think of it, people who don't even know you, are sacrificing themselves so that you can develop a relationship with the Lord. Just like a relationship is a two-way street, by they're doing penance, they're sharing in the weekend with us. This is a visible sign to you personally and to us as a group —that the outside community is not only *praying* for us, but is *doing* penance for us in a variety of ways—just for the sake of a relationship.

Love means giving, not of things, but of the most precious thing we have—ourselves. And that's exactly what these people are doing—they're sacrificing themselves for you and me, so that we might realize the beauty and simplicity that exists in a relationship with God. Viktor Frankl says in his book, *Man's Search for Meaning*: "Suffering ceases to be suffering in some way at the moment it finds a meaning such as the meaning of a sacrifice." (p. 179)

Palanca means to lift ourselves from our mundane existence to a higher ideal, as was so aptly expressed earlier today in the talk on Ideals and Maturity. We can't do it all by ourselves. We need help from our brothers and sisters outside of these walls. It's in their relationship with God, that they

141

*Revelation comes through culture. As Jesus used mud to heal blindness and God used myth to reveal truth, we are called to the creative use of culture. Faith is in life, in play, in dance. It is communicated by living people, dancing, playing and being together.*

are interceding with the Holy Spirit to work in us—to cause a metanoia in us.

In Spanish, another meaning for the word Palanca is "lever" or "steering mechanism" of an airplane. This could be productive of a fresh set of images.


## PASCHAL VIGIL


(For accompanying ritual and ceremony, please see Chapter XI Liturgical and Paraliturgical Ceremonies.)

A. Baptism plunges us into the Paschal Mystery of Christ. (Vatican Council II)

   1. We have experienced the beginning of the Paschal Mystery today.

   2. Speak of fire and water—symbols of Baptism.

B. Fire.

   1. Symbolism.

      a) Destructive—kills, consumes—e.g. "sin papers."

      b) Constructive—gives heat and light.

   2. Christ is the Light of the World.

   3. Christ's light is in us.

   4. Small candles—lit from Paschal Candle (Christ) and extinguished by each person— Light is *in you.*

C. Water.

   1. Symbolism.

      a) Destructive—floods.

b) Constructive—drink, refreshes, cleans.

2. Water in Baptism is symbol of death to life.

3. Early Christians baptized by immersion. Going completely under the water symbolized the new life in Christ.

4. When Christians emerged from the pool of baptism, they put on a long white robe (little white stole used in TEC) to symbolize their new life.

D. Conclusion.

All are invited to renew their baptismal commitment to the Lord.


# SUNDAY


*THE RISEN CHRIST*


A Man Rose Up

He rose from an apparently terrible defeat of all His dreams. His lacerated body on the cross and in the tomb seemed to symbolize all His plans—broken, torn to shreds, a cruel joke. The Savior—He couldn't even save Himself.

His friends, His closest ones, His brethren, they —like all the rest—had scattered. He seemed utterly alone, a dead man in tomb—abandoned.

*But He rose up.* New breath pushed its way through His lungs—His heart began pulsating, warm vibrant blood started to course through His veins. He awakened, opened His eyes in the great darkness. He stood up, the stone rolled away. The light and fresh air came streaming through.

He walked out into the light of the rising sun and stood erect, feet firmly planted on the ground, eyes gazing into the heavens and then His gaze embracing the world around Him. His gentle voice greeted Mary Magdalen who was searching for Him. "Mary, go tell my friends the good news, I am risen."

Jesus, the man, has risen from the dead.

My Jesus, You are truly human—one of us. You are made of the same flesh and blood as we are. You are our brother.

Because you have risen, Jesus, that means I can rise also.

Right now, rising from the dead isn't so important to me. What I seek from you, Jesus, is the power to rise from the discouragement I feel so often, the sadness and depression that weighs me down. Give me strength to rise up and overcome the sense of hopelessness at times especially when I have messed up my life and see no way out.

Jesus, sometimes I feel like I'm in a dark tomb, alone and frightened. I'm not strong enough to push away that heavy stone which keeps me shut in. That stone is so big and heavy—it is made up of so many things: my past sins, my selfishness, my shyness, my lack of love, my worry for the future.

But Jesus, you have risen—you have overcome! You said your strength would always be ours for the asking—wherever you are, we also would be.

Now I can begin to hope you will come and roll away this heavy stone that keeps me locked in the darkness of fear.

I believe I can rise up now because your power and strength are in my limbs, your spirit of courage and joy in my heart.

Jesus, I will arise today, now to walk into the sunlight with you, to breathe the fresh air of your love and live a new life among my friends.

I will rise and sing a song of praise to you with all my brothers and sisters in the name of all creation. I will make my life the glory and vision of the Lord. I praise and thank you, Jesus, for rising up and taking my hand so that I too may truly rise now and at the last day.


## GOD IS A COMMUNITY OF LOVE—OUTLINE

Is God a community of love?

Speak of God—community—love—and then tie in all three.

A. Who is God?

    1. Old Testament

        a) God as Creator.

        b) "I am" Yahweh. (Lev 3:14)

        c) Preserver.

        d) One who called Abraham.

        e) Comforter.

        f) Deliverer.

Examples:  1) Exodus—God as Deliverer, the one with us.
2) Book of Wisdom—God as Wisdom.
3) Prophets—God as one who is to come. God as leader. Prophets knew the times and read the signs of the time.

2. New Testament

a) Christ as Messiah.
b) Lord—"Make ready the way of the...." (Lk 3:4)
c) Father—refer to the Prodigal Son Meditation.
d) Spirit—"the way, and the truth, and the life." (Jn 14:6)
e) Christ "The Word became flesh..." (Jn 1:14)
f) God is love—1 Jn 4:16.

B. Community.

1. Community meaning—come to unity.

a) Acts 2:41-47—common, sharing, concern for others, by being sensitive to others—
1) Ideas.
2) Emotions.
3) Feelings.
4) Ourselves.

2. Community being the Body of Christ.

a) 1 Cor 12:12-31—different parts of the body making up a whole. Relate this to the body being TEC and different parts being the team and the candidates.

   b) Who makes up the Body of Christ? People make up the Body of Christ.

      Example: Karen Horney explains three types of people:

      1) People who: move toward; move against; move away.

      2) We as people who make up the Body of Christ need all three in our lives. We need to share in sensitivity, concern and in life.

## C. Love.

1. God is love—love is God—1 Jn 4:7-21

2. Love as action. Signs of love—a kiss, smile, holding hands. Refer to the Prodigal Son Meditation for different signs of love as described in 1 Cor 13:1-13. Conclude with "Love never fails."

3. No fear in love—Jn 15:12 ff.

   a) "You are my friends"—not slaves. Refer to a relationship of trust, not of mistrust.

   b) Jesus told us "Greater love than this. . . ."

4. Love one another. There cannot be love without people. People love is the same as loving people or loving one another. At least two people make up a community.

## D. Conclusion.

1. God is love. God loved us (His people) first. Where there is love, then there is God. God is love. God is a community of love. Where there is true community there is God.

2. "Put on Love"—Col 3:12-17—which makes

unity, which makes community. GOD-LOVE-COMMUNITY.

## CHRISTIAN LIFE—PIETY

A. Misconceptions of Piety.

Deal with in such a way that they do not prompt the listener to judge what he or she has observed in someone else, but only to examine his own life. The speaker must only point a finger at himself, never at others.

1. "Holy Joes"—appearance is what counts: folded hands, time spent on knees, etc., concerned only for self and not with the salvation of others.

2. Mechanical type—only the "letter of the law" counts, minimum requirements performed out of fear.

3. Hypocritical type—pretend to be what they're not: perform acts of "religion" for human glory.

B. Definition of Christian Piety.

Responding in a living dynamic relationship with the person who is God—knowing, loving, and serving Him.

C. Characteristics of a Life of Piety.

1. Natural—never phony: sincere exterior expression of what is real within. It will have the loving simplicity and confidence of a natural father-child relationship.

2. Courageous—Christianity is failing to the extent that Christians are Christians in secret. "Your light must shine before men...." (Matt 5:16).

3. Mature—the more human I am, the more I am drawn by my ideal, the ideal that motivates me and makes my life worthwhile.

4. Joyful—this discovery of God in my life, the realization that I am His son and He is within me makes me joyful and brings interior peace and happiness. Joy is not to be concerned with pleasure.

D. Piety involves.

1. Knowing—it will be a life based on knowing that I am a son of God, brother of Jesus Christ, and a living vehicle of the Holy Spirit. When I know God, not just know about Him, I see things the way He sees them, that is, what His will is in a situation.

2. Loving—I love that which I know to be most important in my life.

3. Serving—a conscious awareness of my relationship with God as my Father, Christ as my Brother and Savior, and a response through my apostolic life as well as my prayer life.

E. Summary.

If I have invited Christ into my life, part of my response to Him will be to identify with His mission. He promised the Holy Spirit who is the power to make us witnesses to the end of the earth. (Acts 18; Matt. 4:19; John 15:8). In other words, the Christian life is incomplete without the apostolate.

It is not likely that I will love God unless I pray to Him, unless I spend some time with Him as a person.

In the liturgy (worship of God as a community), we encounter our best nourishment for the life of grace, for a deeper and more meaningful Christian life.

Prayer can be spontaneous as well as formal. We can tell God what is on our hearts and minds and listen to Him in His word—Scripture.

We can do this with others—and we have shared prayer.

Invite all to share prayer together in the Chapel.


## CHURCH: THE PEOPLE OF GOD

A. God chose people to be special to Him.

   1. In the Old Testament, God chose Israelites to be His people—People of God (Ex 19:33). Among the people were priests, prophets, leaders.

   2. In the New Testament, God made a new covenant with His people—making us His chosen—People of God.

B. We are members of one Body—Christ's Body. Read 1 Cor. 12:12-31. Everyone has his job in the body.

C. Three basic jobs.

1. Priests—Peter tells us all are a royal priest-
   hood (1 Pet. 2:9-10). As a people of God, we
   are set aside by God to offer sacrifice to Him.
   Baptism and Confirmation make us a chosen
   race called to worship God. Speak of different
   roles in liturgy, the public worship of the
   Church.

2. Prophets—as people of God, we are asked to
   make known to the world the mind and will
   of God by our own spoken word and also the
   unspoken word (witness) of our way of
   life.

3. Leaders—as people of God, we must be willing
   to take on the burden of directing others to
   Christ, of leading the world into His love.

## SIGN

A. Definition.

1. Sign is a symbol or that which might be used
   to convey a meaning, an attitude, or a reality.

2. That which is conveyed could be:
   a) Positive—e.g., long-hair on male to a peer
      —freedom in life style.
   b) Negative—e.g., long-hair on male to a
      parent—threat to one's life style.

3. Three types of signs:
   a) Thing or object signs.
   b) Action or gesture signs.
   c) Union signs.

B. Thing—object signs:

1. Many of these on weekend—water, bell, stole, candle, fire.

2. Other examples—wedding ring, words.

C. Action—gesture signs:

Examples—handshake, a look, raised thumb of hitch-hiker, victory sign of World War II has become peace sign of Vietnamese War.

D. Union signs:

1. Examples—kiss of Judas, kiss of lovers, intercourse—union of love.

2. Church is "bride" of Christ—UNION
Christ is in the Father—UNION
Eucharist—bread and wine—THINGS
Eucharist received by Christians—UNION
Comm-union—"United with" Christ in community.

3. Liturgy—Christian community celebrating oneness.

E. Summary.

We become signs to others (when we return home) of our unity with Christ.

F. Suggestion.

Might ask everyone to go outside or anywhere and find a sign of themselves to present at liturgy.

## PEACE

"Peace is my farewell to you, my peace is my gift to you." (Jn 14:27)

(If singing by the community is desired during this talk, a suggested song is *Peace Song* by Judy O'Sheil found in the *Hymnal for Young Christians,* Vol. 1.)

Dear Lord,

You say you have left us peace, but, tell me, where is it? Is it that piece of paper that two countries have signed saying there shall be no more fighting between them, while other peoples are still killing each other, and while the two countries themselves are still very much prepared to let all hell break loose at the snap of a finger? Is this your peace, Lord? Is this what you have left us?

I can't seem to understand you. It seems as though you say one thing, but yet another exists. You say you have left us peace; however, I still see war, murder and other crime. Right now, I am very much confused. Please explain....

"I do not give it to you as the world gives peace." (Jn 14:27)

Oh, is that it, Lord? Is that what you mean? Now I think I understand. You have left a different kind of peace—an inner peace, a peace we can feel in our hearts, a peace that is very personal.

Yes, Lord, I do understand better. You have left us a real peace—a peace that is ours for the taking. You have given us a peace that does not come from overwhelming feats; but a peace that stems from an involvement with the simple joys and sorrows, the successes and failures of our brothers and sisters.

All of creation is a part of it. It encompasses all the beauty that surrounds us every day of our lives from the smile on someone's face to the sharing and comforting of someone else's sorrows, from the joy that we feel when we're with our loved ones to the joy we feel when we realize we are one with you.

Your peace, our peace, is beautiful, Lord, because it is not just the ceasing of gunshots, but rather a calmness and serenity that comes from the soul.

"Because I go to the Father, and whatever you ask in my name I will do, so as to glorify the Father in the Son." (Jn 14:12-13)

Yes, Jesus, I acknowledge that you have left us physically. It is true that you have returned to the glory of your Father's home, but you have not left us with nothing. You promised us that wherever you are we would also be, if we loved you. And so, you have given us your Body and Blood through which we are able to share with you entirely.

You redeemed us by your sacrificial love and you continue your loving concern for those who are troubled. You never hide from those who seek you nor forsake those who fail to follow you. I thank you Jesus for your spirit of love and strength which you share with us in your peace.

I must truly rejoice and give you praise every moment of my life through both my actions and my words of prayer.

"I will ask the Father and he will give you another Paraclete—to be with you always: the Spirit of truth, whom the world cannot accept." (Jn 14:16-17)

Your Spirit of Truth has come and with it the purpose of my life with you. I have found my place in the Son, Jesus, and my place in your plan for peace. I know that I must communicate the healing and saving love you have shown in your lifetime to all those that I myself encounter.

I must not do it haphazardly, but with a touch of creativity and feeling. Where there is hatred, I must sow love. Where there are wounds, I must give healing. Where there is despair, I must proclaim hope. Where there is darkness, I must shed light.

Lord, when I say these acts that I must perform, I truly believe that they are necessary, if I am to attain total peace with myself, others and you. I realize that I alone cannot move mountains, but I can smile instead of frown, I can listen instead of speak, I can love instead of hate. It is necessary to live your truth of love no matter what the consequences, no matter what the cost.

"The command I give you is this, that you love one another. If you find that the world hates you, know it has hated me before you. If you belong to the world, it would love you as its own; the reason it hates you is that you do not belong to the world." (Jn 15:17-19)

How true it is that people will laugh at me and hate me for trying to love them. But if I sincerely love them, then tolerance is necessary in my acceptance of others. After all, didn't you tolerate all the unjust treatment that was given you?

So too, then, must I be tolerant of the actions of others. I must at times literally turn the other cheek. I must cease to be judgmental and condemnatory. I do not expect to condone wrong-doing, but yet sometimes it will be necessary to tolerate it in my acceptance of people as persons.

If someone will not accept the care and affection I show him, then let me in return give him twice as much love. If someone sneers at me for doing some act of kindness, then let me turn to him, smile, and show the kindness towards him also.

I will try, Lord, to do your will of love, but I ask your strength to persevere when times are bad. For it is through perseverance that anyone will be able to draw himself closer to you in peace.

"The word you hear is not mine; it comes from the Father who sent me." (Jn 14:24)

I hear your words, Lord—you tell us to love, honor and forgive. So now, let me begin with my acceptance of your love and forgiveness for me. Then, in turn, grant me the ability to forgive myself. For how can I expect to forgive those who have hurt me when I cannot even forgive myself?

It is remarkable how often my unforgiving attitude toward others is in reality a reflection of my own disgust with myself. Therefore, let me start with a humble and honest view of myself. In that way, I can become tender, receptive, understanding, and forgiving of others. I need to accept people as valid, significant, worthwhile persons even though they fall at times as I also do.

To love, honor and forgive. This is your message

and you say to keep it in our hearts forever. Certainly it is essential to any happy and fruitful relationship whether it be with our own identity, with others, or with you.

Let us then, Lord, cease to speak now and then, so that we may continue to listen to your word. For it is through listening to your words also, that we will be able to let your peace in us grow always.

"Do not let your hearts be troubled. Have faith in God and faith in me." (Jn 14:1)

Finally, before I close this letter, I must admit that I do not know my future course, but I know where I am now and what I am to do. I am here to serve others, to demonstrate your love and to communicate your healing touch to those who are in need.

I thank you, O God, for the simple joys of life, for the endurance to overcome harder days, for making me a truly significant person, for restoring my identity as a member of your family, and for giving me a taste of what it means to have your peace.

Love always....

LET US REMEMBER: PEACE I LEAVE WITH YOU. MY PEACE I GIVE TO YOU. I AM ALWAYS WITH YOU FOR EVER AND EVER.

# MONDAY

*CONFIDENCE IN CHRIST*

A. Opening.

1. Use a quote from the Good News concerning Christ's invitation to people to become one of His followers and to spread the Good News to all nations.

2. State how we have all been called to share this weekend and to encounter Christ in a very real way.

3. Use the parable of the good seed, explain to the candidates how they are the seeds who have fallen among the good soil.

4. To strengthen this, you may also compare the confidence to the grain of mustard seed.

5. Relate to the candidates your own personal confidence in Christ.
   a) What gives you this confidence?
   b) How does this confidence sustain you in trying times?

B. Conclusion:

1. In the conclusion be brief and remind the candidates that the confidence they shared this weekend can sustain them tomorrow and the rest of their lives, but only if they allow Christ to become real to them.

# UNIVERSAL CALL TO HOLINESS—MARRIED LIFE

A. God calls all. A Christian is someone who knows, among other things, that he has been called, and he believes in his vocation. St. Paul said to the Ephesians (1:4): "God chose us in him before the world began, to be holy and blameless in his sight, to be full of love." Regardless of our vocation, we must constantly stand back, re-evaluate, question our motives and the direction in which we're going.

B. Marriage.

   1. Why get married?

     a) Just a social formality?

     b) Because you really love someone. Love is not a feeling, but a choice—ultimate act of freedom.

   2. Two people marrying confer the sacrament on each other. What is the ceremony about?

     a) Witnessing choice.

     b) Before Christian community.

     c) Celebrating this love as a sign of His love.

     d) Receiving strength through prayers of this community.

   3. Grace of marriage.

     a) Grace as a relationship of divine with human.

     b) Your spouse is the grace of marriage.

     c) Deepen relationship with spouse.

     d) Deepen relationship with God.

   4. Prime relationship must be between husband

and wife, but the couple has support of Christian community at the marriage ceremony and during life.

C. Relationship as a Couple.

Communication—vows begin communication of married life, and a good system of communication is the foundation on which any marriage is built. Communication of:

1. Body—sex as giving self to spouse: symbol of self-giving.
2. Heart—sensitivity to other—true friendship.
3. Mind—unity of ideal and direction of life. The largest problem of communication is to face insensitivity of a spouse in a given situation. Solution:
   a) Regain sensitivity by dying to self-centeredness.
   b) Look at life through the eyes of your spouse.
   c) Active and passive parts of life:
      1) Start full of hopes and dreams.
      2) Things will occur outside your control.
   d) Reaction as a couple to reality will make or break you.
   e) Requires faith and dialogue.

D. Relationship as a family.

1. Children are a gift of God.
2. Not just having them, but being responsible parents, leading them to discover who they are, why they are.

3. Necessity of bringing them to awareness of Christo-centric way of life.

4. Parents are prime educators.

E. Relationship with the community.

1. Family doesn't live in isolation, but is a part of a larger community.

2. We respond to His call—"Love one another as I have loved you." (Jn 15:12)

3. Work in the community—a family is aware that the Lord is witnessed and praised by this activity.

F. Reflections.

1. Wedding Feast at Cana. At their wedding reception, the couple suffers an insufficiency of their resources. Let's call it a dulling of their love—the way some couples just seem to exist together, not really love together. There is nothing left but water. Then Christ intervenes, and the second wine is better than the first. The heart knows how to give without thought of gain. In the beginning it simply knew how to open itself to the joy it might receive.

2. Marriage Cross: Symbol of a Christian marriage.
   a) Cross—sign of Christian.
   b) Rings—sign of marriage.
   c) Christ supports marriage as cross supports rings.
   d) Rings representing marriage are placed where vertical member representing our

relationship to God meets horizontal member representing love of others. Love of God and others meet in marriage.

## UNIVERSAL CALL TO HOLINESS—RELIGIOUS LIFE

A. Why did I become a religious?

   1. Desire to serve and witness.

   2. Desire to find my personal way of saying a total yes to God.

B. The meaning of the vows as the basic structure of religious life.

   1. Celibacy.

      a) Very personal—involves the very "stuff" that make me, me.

      b) The "tender and intimate" sacrifices involved—sexually and emotionally.

      c) The why of it:

     1) Freedom for total service.

     2) Sign of the beauty, purity and sacredness of human life.

     3) Sign of the total love which unites us with God.

2. Poverty—being poor and free of spirit so you can depend wholly on God.
  a) Not grasping at things.
  b) "Holy and happy" insecurity.
  c) Regulated by the community and the individual.
  d) The why of it.
    1) Sign of the call to freedom from things.
    2) Sign of the dependence a Christian must have on God alone.

3. Obedience—attentive listening to God's will (tied in with service).
  a) Leaders and members of a community help person to listen.
  b) The needs of the time and God's people help person to listen.
  c) Not always easy—our self gets in the way.
  d) The why of it.
    1) Concrete sign that God has the last word and not us.
    2) Concrete sign that all Christians are called to spread the Good News of Salvation.

4. Prayer is the foundation of life in Christ. We can only be concrete signs if our relationship with Christ is deep, personal, and concrete.

5. Community life forms the environment in which this life can more easily be lived.
   a) All Christians are called to form a sharing community. Religious are called to share on every level so that their very life style will be a concrete sign of this Christian call.
   b) Not always easy but that is what life is. Love of God and each other is what smooths the way.

## UNIVERSAL CALL TO HOLINESS—SINGLE LIFE—OUTLINE

A. A call to holiness.
   1. We each have a call to holiness.
   2. Each of us must develop our unique calling from God.
B. Importance of single life.
   1. The fact that you are single makes you free to give of yourself—no strings.
   2. Single life is not just an interim period or stagnant time in our life.
   3. We must live our life to the fullest.
      a) Discover what your talents are.
      b) Use all of these talents to do His work.
C. We all give life.
   1. Life is love and love is giving oneself to others.
   2. We must get involved in our community.

I know that some people do intentionally choose the single life as a vocation, especially now-a-days, but as for me there was no noble decision on my part. I don't consciously recall ever having decided to be single.

I know that there were factors that led me here, and I could suppose this or that, but I really can't point to any one thing as positively the reason for not marrying or entering the religious life. A married cousin of mine insists that it was just "dumb luck."

Well maybe that is the truth of it, but whatever the reason, here I am, and I would like to share with you, how it was and how it is for me, one single person, as I try to follow Christ daily. And so, may I say:

Single, smingle, can't seem to fuss too much with that.
I am woman and that is that.
I breathe, I eat, I laugh, I cry.
I give, I need, I love, want, and I will die.
I am daughter, I am sister, mother, aunt, lover and friend.

When it is necessary, hopefully I will be strong.
When it is time, forgive me I bend.
Old maid, poor grade—
Reverse, Reverse—
No such thing in God's universe.
I love you...you love me.
I think that puts me in a "Capital D"

166

Divine Category.

I am my Maker's Choice... A fact in which
I do rejoice.
I live my life as best I can...I love my life,
because I am.

When I say "Single, smingle, can't seem to fuss
too much with that" I am saying that the fact
I am single has never been the dominating feeling
in my life. The fact that I am a woman is what
moves me and the fact that I have been introduced
to the teachings of Jesus, God's truth, is what
guides me, when I have the sense to take the
guidance.

I do breathe, eat, laugh and cry...I do give, need,
love, want and surely I will die. I am daughter,
sister, mother, aunt, lover and friend.

As for the "I do's," well frankly, I really haven't
noticed any difference between the way I do the
do's and the way others, not single, do the do's.
However, as I go along doing the do's being a
Christian, I can't help but be aware of when I've
done them right and when I've done them wrong.
The truth can hurt, but why would I want to lie
to myself anyway.

As for the "I am's," there is, of course, a difference in some of the role playings, because I am
single. Nonetheless, these roles are a part of the
single life. Time seems to be a very important factor. Being single allows much more time to be all
of these, when we are called upon. This extra
allowance can be a means to good, used wisely, or
an instrument of hurt, if abused. Because I have
been made aware of this, I ask that when it is
necessary, I will be strong.

167

And then there come the many times, when forgive me, I bend. I do bend. I am weak. I do make a terrible mess of things. It is difficult to accept this weakness, when you feel the need to be perfect. But Christ forgives. If I am to be more Christlike, I must follow Him and try to forgive myself. And so, I go on working. I go on trying and hope that the victory is in the trying.

And then we come to: "Old maid, poor grade—Reverse, Reverse—No such thing in God's Universe."

Unenlightened society tends to label persons who do not fit into what they consider the normal life style. But these are written by imperfect men. Therefore, why should I call them true? I look to God for my label. No one can take away from me what He tells me I am, and what I know I am. Put no tags on me. I am not for sale. Once you realize your true identity, a Child of God, no one can call you less. You walk with pride, dignity, hope and joy.

"I love you...you love me...the Divine Category." Love and loving reaches across all borders. It doesn't matter who you are. As long as the gates of your mind and heart are open, it finds room to live and grow. Love I find is a Divine quality and Divine love fills life with the most necessary and the most rewarding dimension. There is great beauty and peace in the giving and receiving of love. There is great pain and chaos when love is absent. And so, being a practical woman, as best I can, I choose to love.

"I am my Maker's choice, and that does make me rejoice." The fact that God has chosen to allow me to live and to experience all that I have spoken of before, fills me with a feeling of awe. Of course, being only human, there are times when I think I would like to chuck the whole thing.

But in the end, after God sustains me through the hard times, I'm glad He didn't let me. The experience of living here, with all of its beauty, all its pain, and all its love, and the promise of eternal life in God's love, is God's gift to us, the one we all need—the gift of joy.

"I live my life as best I can." Being single usually presents somewhat the same problems and opportunities as all people experience, but they come to us in different ways and on different roads from those travelled by married people or those in the religious life.

However, it does seem, that for the greater part of our lives, no great demands are made on us or on our time. And dare anyone interfere with this. My own personal motto was, "Well here's to you, and here's to me, and here's to hope we both agree. But if we don't, well the hell with you and here's to me." This way of life can really be funsville, and so comfortable, and so dangerous.

But funsville, it turns out, is a town and not a life. And so, there comes a time when either by choice or circumstances, we find ourselves in the larger city of life. Unlike those who have said yes to the religious or married state, our duties are not always set down before us. At first we can really feel like strangers in this big city. We don't know exactly where to go or what to do. But since we have accepted the move, in effect said "yes" to Christ, we learn.

169

We learn that all kinds of people need us and want us—our families, our friends, our co-workers, strangers, children, the young and the old. They've all been waiting for us to arrive. They have so much to tell us, so much to give us, so much need of us. We learn to make ourselves available to them in love, by just being there—where they are—and where we are. And one thing leads to another and we find ourselves, living our life as best we can.

It's true, we all travel different roads in life, but in the end, we are all trying to reach the same goal. I believe its name is fulfillment. Fulfillment is completing ourselves. It is filling ourselves to the brim with what we need to make us whole. Being humans, with a knowledge of God, complete goodness in us, nothing else can really satisfy us. We can only be happy, when Christ lives in us and when we live in Christ.

The next big question is: How can we arrive at this state of fulfillment? Well long before the Triple A Club, God knew that man needed direction. And so He sent out a map leading directly to Him. He said: "Turn right, love God. Then make another right turn, love your neighbor as yourself. And there you are—fulfillment."

The road can be rough and the trip exhausting. But where do we want to go, and where shall we go, if not there?

I do love my life. No wonder at that. God is— I am.

A. The Spiritual Director giving this talk should try to tie in the talks which have preceded this —especially the Church—The People of God— or any talk which ties in with this talk.

B. Jesus told them this parable: "The reign of God is like yeast which a woman took and kneaded into three measures of flour. Eventually the whole mass of dough began to rise." (Mt. 13:33)

Images:

1. Kingdom—is now and will be completed.

2. Dough—our community, our world.

3. Yeast—we must be like yeast as God's people.
    —we must help the "dough"—our community, our world, to rise.
    —yeast works.
    —we should raise up our world by our very presence.
    —others later on will tell us how to be yeast in the world (talks: Christianity in Action and Beyond TEC).

C. We are going out to the world today. When Jesus sent forth His disciples, He told them: "Be on your way and remember I am sending you as lambs in the midst of wolves." (Lk 10:3)

1. Not everyone "out there" is a wolf—but as His disciples, we have become lambs.

2. If wolves come upon us, be prepared. Don't change into a wolf yourself.

*The Easter mystery presented in a way sensitive to the teenage candidates is only two-thirds of what makes TEC effective. The final characteristic, the all-pervasive element, is a faithful dependence on God, who draws people to himself, who opens hearts, who gives faith.*

D. Jesus told us what he wants us to do for one another in the world: "If I washed your feet— I who am Teacher and Lord—then you must wash each other's feet. What I just did was to give you an example: as I have done, so you must do. I solemnly assure you, no slave is greater than his master; no messenger outranks the one who sent him. Once you know all these things, blest will you be if you put them into practice." (Jn 13:14-17)
As "yeast" and "lambs" we must minister to one another.

E. Further thoughts may be obtained from the "Church in the Modern World"—document from Vatican II.


## CHRISTIANITY IN ACTION

A. Awareness of self—aware of the tools and gifts Christ has given to us.

B. Uniqueness of personality—self-acceptance.

C. Christ has accepted you. Accept the fact of your acceptance.

D. Change follows—two types:

   1. Self-revolution—a fundamental change or alteration of attitudes within ourselves, produced by time and effort, leading to a personal commitment to Christ.

   2. Evolution—a gradual development or growth. Both changes should be rooted in Christ.

E. This change in us demands action—personal action is not enough. We must act or work in institutions, groups, clubs, and agencies that affect persons. Give examples.

F. Avenues that exist for Christian action.

1. Our own home.
2. Poverty programs.
3. Catholic Youth Organization.
4. Young Christians Students.
5. Candy stripers (hospital volunteers).
6. Nursing homes.
7. Scouting.
8. CCD.
9. Prayer groups.
10. Any other examples.

G. Types of work being done.

1. Social action: recreation, tutoring, homework center, Big Brother, scouting, etc.
2. Religious action: teach CCD, lectors and commentators, guitar masses, etc.
3. Hospital work: aged, handicapped, etc.

H. Conclusion: Get where the action is!

*BEYOND TEC*

Another suggested reading: *That Man is You*, Louis Evely, Cp. 7, Lay Spirituality, pp. 199-204.

A. Remeeting family.

Although the parents have been informed by mail of what is involved in TEC, nevertheless they may not be prepared for the return of the "Prodigal Child" full of eagerness to convince them that the only way to celebrate liturgy is with guitars and hand clapping. Discuss TEC, but *don't* be overpowering.

B. Remeeting friends.

The real danger is coming on too strong. Don't try to coerce them into making TEC. It is actions (especially lasting actions) rather than words that will most influence them.

C. De-briefing sessions.

Give details of de-briefing sessions in various areas.

D. Future TEC functions.

The TEC weekend is just what it says—an encounter with Christ. In order to make this encounter more lasting and meaningful, there are certain follow-up activities which help to recharge and revitalize the TEC community. Stress the importance of attendance at the reunions (especially the one for the specific TEC), and future Hootenannies. Also point out the need for palanca for future TECs—the monthly Newsletter will give dates and other information. Local reunions have been set up at various centers and attendance at these should be encouraged.

E. The surprise element.

This aspect is an intimate part of the TEC weekend and when talking to prospective candidates it may be best to discuss the weekend in generalities rather than the specifics. Do *not* bring potential candidates to hootenannies or reunions.

F. Team and TEC Council.

If any of the candidates are interested in being team members on future TECs, or if they wish to serve on any of the various subcommittees of the TEC Council, contact should be made with a member of the Council. It may be necessary to briefly explain the workings of the Council.

G. Conclusion.

It should be stressed that the team members are available at all times to meet with and talk to the candidates, if required.

# 11
# Liturgical
# Ceremonies

During the course of the TEC weekend, four sacraments are experienced. The sacraments of Initiation—Baptism and Confirmation—are paraliturgical, that is, they are experienced in the form of a renewal. The sacraments of Penance and Eucharist are liturgical—Penance being celebrated on Saturday evening and Eucharist on Sunday and Monday. These sacraments will be considered in the order of their occurrence during the weekend.

## A. PENANCE

All of the talks on Saturday pave the way for the experience of the sacrament of Penance. There is the talk on the sacrament itself, the meditation on the Prodigal Son, and the personal "Metanoia" talk. All of these set the mood for the celebration of the sacrament. At a signal from the Lay Director, all the priests leave for the assigned areas where they will celebrate Penance. Since this period is not very long, the candidates should be instructed beforehand in the talks about the difference between confession and counselling. Counselling can, if necessary, be done at this time—but should be deferred until a point in the schedule which leaves the priest more time to do so. This observation is made, not so much from a numerical viewpoint, but moreso from the nature of the sacrament of healing.

The celebration of Penance can be done in the ordinary way or it can be enhanced by communal involvement. The Church has urged community celebrations of this sacrament, and the Spiritual Directors are encouraged to prepare a penance service (e.g., bible readings, psalms, songs) for the candidates. However, this is not essential to the weekend.

## B. SERVICE OF ASHES (OPTIONAL)

In the spirit of the season of Lent, this service could contribute to the development of the theme for Saturday. The same experience of the Church on Ash Wednesday is repeated in this service. Ashes from palm may be used. Ashes from a burning during the weekend itself may also be used.

## C. PASCHAL VIGIL SERVICE

The last event on the Saturday schedule is the Paschal Vigil Service. It is most fittingly held in the chapel area. In essence, there is a talk followed by burning of sin papers and lighting of the paschal candle (both optional at this time, see Detailed Schedule, Chapter VIII, Saturday, Nos. 18 and 19.) Next the candidates are invited to renew their baptismal vows. Three Spiritual Directors are needed at this time. (The Lay Director or Assistant Director can assist as needed.) Each candidate and team member is given a small candle which is lighted from the paschal candle. On the altar is a small container of water, a towel, and small white stoles (enough for all present).

Each person who comes forth is asked to extinguish the small candle and hand it to the first Spiritual Director. As this is done, the Spiritual Director tells the person: "Remember, NAME, you are now the light of Christ and the light is in you." The person moves to the second Spiritual Director who places a few drops of water on the candidate's head saying: "Remember, NAME, you must die in order to live." Then the person approaches the third Spiritual Director who places a white stole around the neck and says: "NAME, receive this stole as the sign of the Christ-life in you."

Once this is completed, a period of prayer and/ or a simple song of new life and joy can end the service.


D.  EUCHARIST


The sacrifice of the Mass is celebrated on Sunday afternoon and as the last event on Monday.

Liturgy on Sunday follows the "Sign" talk and should be led by the Spiritual Director who has given the "Sign" talk. The Lord's presence in His Word and each other should have been experienced by this time. The presence of the Lord in His Body and Blood should be shared and the Eucharist reserved in the chapel for the remainder of the weekend. A Spiritual Director should speak about the Eucharistic presence and invite everyone to visit the chapel during the remainder of the weekend.

A suggestion for the Sunday liturgy is to ask everyone to find a sign of themselves from nature or anywhere and to have them present these at some point in the liturgy. They should explain the sign and these can be placed on or around the altar for Mass. This has been done as the homily for this Mass and the thoughts from the "Sign" talk become real to the candidates.

Eucharist on Monday should take its theme from the mission of the community to go forth and be witnesses to Jesus. (Eucharist in reservation should be consumed at this Mass.) Within this liturgy, the community can be encouraged to renew the sacrament of Confirmation. This can be done after communion. (See Detailed Schedule, Chapter VIII, Monday, No. 13.) A brief exhortation on the sacrament of Confirmation, on the imposition of hands, together with a reading from Scripture (e.g., Acts 2) is suggested. After the candidate has been invested with his TEC cross by the Lay Director, the Spiritual Directors can impose hands on everyone individually.

## E.  LITURGY FOR HOOTENANNY

Eucharist can be celebrated for those who will be attending the hootenanny on Sunday. This should be a celebration apart from the Eucharist for the candidates and team. A former Spiritual Director can celebrate this liturgy of the particular Sunday. It can be celebrated before or after the hootenanny. An advantage of celebrating the Eucharist before is the tone it sets for the hootenanny. The larger TEC community can prepare themselves for the joyful experience of the hootenanny.  Moreover, everyone can return home earlier.


## F.  CHAPEL VISITS

After the "Piety" talk on Sunday morning, the community is invited to make its first chapel visit together. Once this happens, the Lay Director or a Spiritual Director can encourage all to visit individually or in table groups. "Table" visits become a force for cohesion towards community.


## G.  MEAL PRAYER

Each table (including and starting with the director's table) can be assigned to prepare "grace" for a particular meal during the weekend. Freedom, originality, and spontaneity should be stressed.

We have grown up enough, have gained enough faith and confidence to free us from fear of "losing the young people." We have learned that it is God who draws all of us to himself and that we need not bribe anyone. God will use us during the TEC weekend and after if we open ourselves to his loving direction.

# 12
# Follow-Up

The TEC weekend is a spiritual and emotional introduction to the Christian life of belief and love. The three days of TEC, as an introduction (pre-evangelization), cannot be expected to be more than a preparation for the planting of a seed of faith. The later stages of evangelization and catechesis plant and nurture the Lord's seed. This is the responsibility of each Christian community. The TEC community takes a part in this work through the on-going structure of the weekends. This has been called the follow-up program.

## A. HOOTENANNY

The Hootenanny is the most common feature of the TEC follow-up. Here, the gathering of past TECers for the benefit of the TEC in progress is a true community-building event. The uplifting song and the spiritual food of the peace talk serve to strengthen the young Christians in their new belief. The hootenanny is a joyful celebration into which the seriousness of long teachings and the soul-searching necessary for the Christian life should not be injected. The joy of the hootenanny is crucial to the candidates of the TEC in progress, and the spiritual needs of the larger community must be subservient to the need for celebration. Thus, the hootenanny, as a follow-up tool, presents a number of limitations. The Christian life is more than joyous celebration. It is the struggle of the flesh and the spirit. It is penance. It is discipline and sensitivity. Our young people must be witnessed to, instructed, and challenged concerning commitment, morality, and social action. The hootenanny is not the proper forum for this and a series of reunions have evolved.

## B. *GENERAL REUNIONS*

General reunions are held two weeks after the hootenanny. Originally, these were held for the previous TEC alone, but as a response to the need for teaching and prayer, the reunion is now open to the entire TEC community. The TECers from the last TEC meet privately an hour before the general reunion begins.

During this hour, they are able to renew acquaintances, celebrate the song, witness to one another what has gone on in their lives, and share scripture and prayer. They then join the larger community and together all participate in the program for that reunion.

Below is a list of programs of some of the TEC reuhions:

1. Presentation and discussion on knowing the will of God; Liturgy.

2. Teaching given by Jose Gomez on the Lettuce Boycott and the plight of the migrant worker; Liturgy.

3. Special Christmas reunion, extended liturgy, Christmas tree-trimming at offertory, Christmas peace talk, seasonal music throughout.

4. Teaching on Man by Rabbi Erwin Zimmet; Liturgy.

5. Teaching on Christian Spirituality by Father Thomas Hopko, Pastor of Russian Orthodox Church; Liturgy.

6. Prayer: Teaching and small prayer meeting led by a local prayer group leader who directed TEC 3; Liturgy.

7. Presence of Jesus
   a) Scripture sharing in small groups for liturgy of the word.
   b) Eucharist—film on presence in the Eucharist.
   c) The sharing of His presence in each other.

8. Multi-media Liturgy.

Reunions are planned by the follow-up committee consisting of TECers and adults. From this general committee came a number of smaller, local committees set up to plan local reunions.

## C. *LOCAL REUNIONS*

Local reunions have been a good forum for teaching and sharing on a personal level. Local committees have sponsored vigils throughout the night as palanca for TEC weekends. Because of their grass-roots involvement they have made the Spirit of the Lord pervade their own groups and committees. Local groups can also capitalize more upon the events of the liturgical calendar without the need for long trips or the disruption of family plans. For example, the New York City local committee sponsored a sunrise liturgy on Easter Sunday. The TEC community was able to celebrate the Lord's Resurrection together and still be close to home.

## D. *WEEKLY MEETINGS AND DE-BRIEFING*

Local groups have held weekly meetings where TECers can share in liturgy and Christian fellowship. A special type of local gathering has come to be known as the "de-briefing." A de-briefing takes place on Monday evening (usually in a home) when TEC has finished. Former TECers and team members gather and candidates and team who have just completed their TEC are encouraged to come to the de-briefing to share about their experience. Many are usually very vocal at this time and their enthusiasm can be both appreciated and absorbed by people who have had a similar experience. This makes "re-entry" into home, school, and community a bit easier. Prayer is often shared during this time.

## E.  PARENTS' NIGHT

Another event that can and should take place in various localities is called a "Parents' Night." This simply means that parents of TECers are invited to a home to share with adults who have been on TEC teams and with other TECers. The program can be one of talks, discussions, and even skits. This type of function gives parents a better chance to understand TEC and possibly become involved themselves.

## IMPORTANT:

*The task of keeping the salt flavorsome and the light shining is truly a difficult one.  Our young people cannot be fed sufficiently by TEC alone no matter how extensive the follow-up. TEC, as a program, is worthless unless it be in organic union with the Body of Christ and in prayerful and faithful dependence on Jesus Himself. Without Him no program, no plan, no organization can work. Yet with our eyes on the Lord, TEC can build up the Body and give it the power of Jesus.*

*Knowing Jesus the way we do, having experienced the new life that emerges when the good news of the Gospel becomes our own good news, it is natural that we should continue to celebrate in the follow-up hootenanny.*

# 13
# TEC
# Council

As a TEC community grows, so also does its needs. To respond to these needs, a Council can be formed. Its prime function would be to assume the administrative, financial, and planning requirements of the program. The Council members can be selected from a cross-section of the TEC community; male and female, teens and adults, lay and religious, from all sections of the diocese.

Each Council member should have some previous TEC experience either as a candidate or a team member. The essential requirement for Council members would be a commitment to TEC and a strong desire to serve the Lord. Serving on the Council is a very real form of ministry—it is doing the Lord's work to help spread His word.

The TEC Council could be structured so as to insure that all aspects of the program are given necessary attention. This structure remains flexible so as to change when the need changes. This is also true as regards the size of the Council. It can be divided into committees with Council members serving as chairperson. Each chairperson can, at his or her discretion, select from the community individuals to assist them in performing the committee work. Committee members can be selected from outside the TEC community when individuals can provide professional services in a special field (e.g., advertising, accounting, administration, etc.).

## A. COMMITTEES

1. Applications—distribution of application forms, receiving applications, checking on sponsors, sending out candidate acceptance letters (the acceptance of a candidate is solely in the hands of this committee), and receiving and delivering palanca.

2. Publicity—spread the word about TEC by distributing literature, brochures; arranging for candidate recruitment in schools, CCD, etc; preparing to give talks for recruitment and studying the means which can be used to spread the word.

3. Follow-up—plan and arrange reunions and hootenannies, arrange for speakers, themes and teachings, study and implement means to keep TEC alive within the community.

4. Supplies/Facility—procure all supplies such as pads, pencils, crosses, Good News, posters and all other materials required for TEC weekends; arrange for facilities for weekends, hootenannies, and reunions, proper coverage for kitchen palanca.

5. Correspondence—maintain communication with the TEC community via notices, announcements and a newsletter, be a focal point for all correspondence between committees and community, keep the community informed.

6. TEC Centers—liaison between local TEC center and TEC centers throughout the United States; establish communications to exchange ideas, experience and events; link all geographic locations as a single community.

7. Music—coordinate all TEC music, insure availability of musicians for all TECs' reunions, and hootenannies; establish a legal, copyrighted songbook for use at all TEC events and prepare musical program for same. Keep prayer in song alive and well.

8. REC—arrange and coordinate the program in correctional institutions. Make appropriate contacts and insure all requirements are met to bring Christ to those behind locked doors.

## B. *OFFICERS*

In addition to the committees, the Council has two officers:

1. Chairman—arrange Council meetings, prepare agenda and conduct meetings; act as official Council representative when required; serve the Council members in whatever capacity is needed.

2. Secretary—take minutes of Council meetings, prepare and mail prior to next meeting; contact Council members of events relative to Council

activity; assist chairman in area of records, correspondence and mailings.

Though the Council is divided into many committees, it functions mainly as a single body. It has the responsibility of selecting the Lay Director for each TEC weekend. Once the director is selected, the Council in no way interferes with the selection of the team or the course of the weekend. This remains in the hands of the Lay Director. The Council relieves the team of all details and insures they are covered completely.

The Council evaluates each TEC and all associated activities. In planning for succeeding weekends, it utilizes the experience gained through evaluations and attempts to improve where necessary. When needs of the program arise, the Council acts to fill them.

The Council primarily serves the complete TEC community. It works for the community and attempts to make itself as invisible as possible. Though the Council does make decisions, the decisions are directed to make TEC grow and flourish. Its members are dedicated and committed to help plant the seed of Christ in fertile ground.

# 14
# Residents
# Encounter
# Christ

We would like to express our inadequate thanks for the overwhelming gifts of love, faith, and prayer you have tendered to us all. We felt we were pretty well insulated to and from public approval and disapproval in here, yet we all accepted the challenge of this REC program, thereby opening a chink in our armor of selfishness and deceit.

The inspiration of your efforts is better expressed by our reactions rather than empty words. Thirty felons were transformed into vulnerable human beings as we read your notes and offerings for the success of our venture. More than one voice was husky with emotion as we shared the countless testimonies of your genuine love for us all.

While we accepted Christ as a living force within us, you could see hardened countenances soften into the innocence and compassion for others that our mothers saw there when we made our First Communion so many years ago. The closing prayer in the evening was supplemented by whispered thanks for the new love and insight we now are beginning to recognize.

When the Our Father was concluded we spontaneously offered each other the sign of peace.

We humbly wish to offer the Peace of the Lord to all

of you and yours with a heartfelt thank you and a solemn
God bless.

## A.  RESIDENTS ENCOUNTER CHRIST

REC (Residents Encounter Christ—a term coin-
ed by the inmates of Greenhaven Correctional Facility, Stormville, New York) is the entire TEC program as described in this manual which can be used in jails, prisons, or other types of correctional
facilities. To date, RECs have been conducted in
Massachusetts at the Lawrence County Jail, Lawrence; in Walpole Prison, Walpole; in New York
at the Greenhaven Correctional Facility, Stormville; in Bedford Hills Correctional Facility (for
women), Bedford Hills; and in Fishkill Correctional
Facility, Beacon.

We include this chapter on REC so as to encourage
such a program to be conducted in other facilities and also to include items which pertain more
specifically to the REC program as an outgrowth
of TEC.

The REC program is appropriate for the inmates
of correctional institutions for the following reasons:

1. The majority of inmates have a religious
   maturity comparable to that of the people
   which the TEC program serves.

2. The average stay in prison is being increas-
   ingly reduced and over 90% of the people in
   prison will come out eventually. Therefore,

194

most inmates are at a crossroads in their
lives—calling for decisions about their future—very similar to the TEC candidates.

3. Similar to teens, the inmate is a ward and
relatively free from the pressure of deciding about the near future regarding such
things as meals, clothes, and lodging.

## B. PROBLEMS

The problems involved in the implementation of
the REC program are threefold:

1. The prison structure.
2. The prison system.
3. The inmate mentality.

### 1. *The Prison Structure*

Most prisons have very uncomfortable accom-
modations—especially if the team remains overnight. Food and lodging for a team are difficult
to set up. A conference room and table and chairs
are needed. Good chapel and meditation areas
are difficult to obtain. Finally, distracting noises
and disturbances are often experienced because the
REC cannot be suitably isolated.

### 2. *The Prison System*

Adapting to a time schedule that is right almost
to the point of remaining unchangeable creates further complications. There are interruptions for visits
and institutional appointments. There is limited
time for personal encounter due to the schedule for
inmates' meals, "counts," and evening lock-in. The

Some inmates will attend an REC weekend for a break in their routine. Motivation of this type should not be cause for concern. It is not WHY an inmate participates that is important; it is the fact that he participates at all.

system at times frustrates follow-up by the team both on an individual and group level.

Because the prison is a parish, the chaplain may consider the team as "outsiders." There may be a tendency to overprotectiveness on the part of the chaplain.

During the REC, it is necessary to adhere to all rules and regulations of the prison system for ease of operation and for congenial encounters with prison personnel—guards, administrators, chaplains.

## 3. *The Inmate Mentality*

It will be noted that some inmates will attend a REC weekend for a break in their routine. Motivation of this type should not be a cause for concern, for it matters not *why*, as much as *the fact that* an inmate participates in the weekend. It should be noted, however, that sincerity is sometimes difficult to gauge because of the inmate's ability to "con."

Also, a deep-seated distrust of authority figures —priests, teachers, lecturers, outsiders—will also permeate the inmates. There is a tendency, moreover, for the inmate to want to discuss his court case rather than participate in the discussion at hand. The subject of discussion should be resumed, but as gently as possible.

The inmate may exhibit the feeling that Christian concern is only on the spiritual level, but Christianity in action will be evident throughout the weekend, in the talks, and in the follow-up activities.

Finally, although inmates live together, there is

no sense of community. Some inmates may get to know other inmates for the first time during the weekend.

## C. *SELECTION OF TEAM*

Spiritual Directors and Lay Directors should be familiar with TEC. It would be beneficial if they have experience in working with minority groups, if they are bi-lingual—Spanish, Italian, or any other language. They must, like the rest of the team, be adaptable to the restrictions of the institution.

The Lay Director must keep to a strict time-table. Moreover, the Lay Director should be able to get support of the larger Christian community as regards palanca, baked goods, etc. Team members should be solid people who also have had previous TEC experience. This last point is important because previous TEC experience helps cut down on the problems that could possibly arise from persons serving on team for the first time.

Where possible, inmates (former RECers) should be chosen for team. They should be given one of the talks and there should be meetings, if possible, with the complete team—"outsiders" and inmates.

## D. *FOLLOW-UP*

Both Lay Director and team should be prepared to plan and participate in follow-up. The date for the formal reunion should be agreed on before the weekend begins and revealed to the inmates during the course of the weekend.

Arrangements should be made for visiting and writing—always being sensitive to the rules.

A strong sense that the weekend is not the end of the association should be left with the inmates. Finally, spiritual assistance should be made available to a released inmate from the Christian community, especially in the form of reunions, prayer meetings, hootenannies, etc.

## E.  RESOURCE

Anyone interested in more details about any aspect of the REC program may obtain them by contacting:

> Mr. Thomas Rubeo
> RD 6 Heaton Lane
> Wappingers Falls, New York 12590
> 914-226-6523

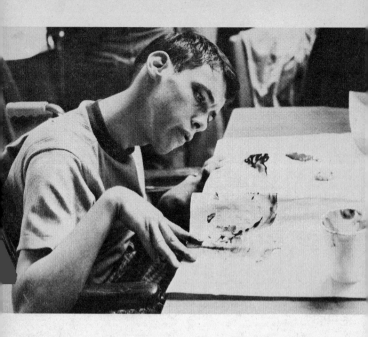

*HEC exists because society labels individuals as "handicapped." Such labels dehumanize and so the weekend experience must be remembered and new experiences offered the deaf, the blind and the lame to help them to see themselves as valuable humans with great gifts to give the world.*

# 15
# Handicapped
# Encounter
# Christ

Within the last ten years there has finally come alive an interest and deep concern for the education of special children, among whom are physically disabled children. Physically disabled adults have begun to make their needs known to American society.

They have joined the ranks of numerous minority groups whose rights have been neglected in the cry for recognition and equality. They struggle with valor. The whole physically disabled populace is now making its presence felt.

Long before these past ten years I felt intensely, the plight of the physically disabled. For many summers I worked with crippled children as counselor and camp director. This was enlightening, challenging, and life-directing.

Then, years later, I found myself confined to a wheelchair for two years and experienced the impact of severe physical disability. Those experiences, coupled with positive, profound religious experiences have led to my present beliefs about physically disabled people; and what positive effects meaningful religious experiences can have in their lives.

While disabled myself, I found that I was separated from the rest of society and that my whole personality underwent an unexpected change. People treated me differently, I responded differently, and I began to see myself as a less than whole human being.

Fortunately, I finally recognized what was happening to them. When I was able to walk again, and had participated in a number of profound retreat experiences, I decided to do all in my power to share similar religious experiences with the disabled, in hopes that they, too, might recognize what disability did to their lives. Thus, HEC was born.

This chapter gathers and summarizes all available information concerning HEC. The impact on people's lives, however, cannot be summarized. This also is an opportunity to describe the program for those interested in working with the disabled in retreat programs.

Perhaps this program or parts of it will fill human needs somewhere. Two great human needs are *to communicate,* and *to generate a positive self-image.* Hopefully this chapter indicates that HEC can meet these two needs in profound ways.

# INTRODUCTION

*Handicapped Encounter Christ* (*H.E.C.*) is a three and one half day religious retreat experience not officially sanctioned or associated with an organized church, but principally Roman Catholic in worship expression.

It is designed to meet the physical, spiritual and (when possible) the emotional needs of physically disabled youth and adults. The weekend is not designed specifically to meet the needs of those individuals whose primary disability is mental retardation.

This chapter will attempt to describe the Handicapped Encounter Christ program. An important part of this chapter gives a detailed account of the schedules, details, flavor of the weekend.

Those who have participated in the HEC weekend experience have ranged in age from fourteen to eighty-seven, and display a variety of disabilities including cerebral palsy, polio, blindness, multiple scelerosis, muscular dystrophy, congenital birth defects, strokes, epilepsy, traumatic accidents and deafness. Therefore, the unique design of the weekend is an important part of a description of HEC, as well as being crucial to the understanding of the responses.

## ATTITUDES TOWARD HANDICAPPED

In America's multi-level, competitive fast-paced society, a concept of wholeness is closely linked with superior physical and mental abilities. Deviation from socially held ability norms is seldom tolerated. Individuals, are categorized and labeled because of sex difference, physical dexterity, intellectual functioning and physical appearance.

The Ideal American becomes a handsome well-proportioned, well-coordinated, alert, well dressed individual whose thoughts and behaviors never push the outer limits of the "conventional". Such outward symbols as "the right toothpaste", attendance at the "good schools," reverence for the free enterprise system, and the willingness with which he or she swears to produce an exact replica of what already exists, are all part of being a whole person within our society.

Within this culture, some provisions have been made for those who are deviant. Individuals whose behavior differs greatly from socially determined norms are placed either in mental institutions or prisons. Those whose ideas differ too radically are labeled as spies, criminals, or misfits. In like manner, and even more acutely differentiating, is physical difference.

Physical difference has historically been cause for extreme reaction by the larger society. Black skin or a large nose, for example, can immediately consign people to undesired social categories which place great pressures for expected behavior on them. These predetermined assumptions frequently are so strong that the "truth" of the assumptions *becomes a hurtful belief for those on whom it has been imposed.*

The attitude of society toward the physically

disabled is in many ways more handicapping than the disability itself. Society claims recognition of worth, empathy with the plight of the disabled, and solicitous treatment of those with physical anomalies, but in fact, makes them totally useless within that society which pretends to care.

Several approaches have been used and continue to be used when dealing with the "problem" of the physically handicapped. One striking approach effectively used in Nazi Germany, was simply to eliminate those who were physically or mentally disabled! Even today, many Americans assume that the disabled are less than whole persons.

The Anglo-American approach has been to lump similar disabilities into educational groups and/or programs, then proceed to educationally define what each group's capacities or capabilities might be. For example, blind are frequently encouraged to express any musical talents, and perhaps because of their mobility despite the loss of vision, are generally considered to have equal, if not superior intellectual ability.

The deaf, on the other hand, because of their inability to speak clearly, and obvious difficulty with communication skills, are often assumed incapable of real contribution to society in general and often are labeled retarded. Blind or deaf individuals can, however, move easily from place to place, so for that and other reasons can be considered to some, a novelty or oddity. These are people about whom some say, "Oh, yes, I knew one once."

Physically disabled who are motorically impaired

pose multiple problems. They are noticeable. A faltering gait, a wheel chair, or an inability to keep still at appropriate times is associated with lack of intellectual capacity, and therefore also associated with lack of ability to contribute.

Deviant or handicapped individuals seem to be consistently categorized so as to negate the possibility for individuality. For the purposes of this chapter it seems important to distinguish between the terms *handicapped* and *disabled*.

A *disability* is something which prohibits manual or intellectual dexterity and is an inconvenience when one wishes to function at a given task. A *handicap* is closely related to a physical, mental or emotional disability. A handicap prevents the individual from dealing with, or adjusting to a disability.

If we use the above definitions, a large percentage of the total population is disabled and/or handicapped. Actual physical disability and the ensuing handicaps have been for many a much more debilitating process than should be necessary in society if individual differences and contributions were truly accepted and treasured.

"Disability appears to be as much a problem for the non-disabled majority as it is for the disabled minority. Maladjustment in normal individuals with respect to physical disability is widespread. However, we cannot change our society overnight, and social attitudes often present problems that can be dealt with only indirectly.

"It appears that a dead end has been reached. If disability is relatively fixed, and society is relatively inflexible, that leaves only the person."[1]

---

1 William M. Cruickshank. ed., *Psychology of Exceptional*

As a youngster or adult continues living with a disability, the treatment that he or she receives from those around him contributes to a self-fulfilling prophecy.[2] If for a long enough period of time an individual is expected to behave in certain patterns, he will in fact behave in those patterns, and most damaging of all, he will come to believe that this is how he *should* behave, and that this is the only way in which he is capable of behaving. The self image of such individuals is generally severely distorted; frequently a positive self image is almost non-existent.

For the more severely physically disabled or for those who have multiple disabilities, institutionalization is sometimes necessary or desired by families. But the process of long-term institutionalization frequently has devastating emotional and physical effects.[3]

The problems of public financial aid, architectural barriers, or the legal rights of deviant individuals are secondary concerns within the framework of HEC's goals: to be accepted, respected, and considered as a whole person, as one is, while at the same time presenting an environment in which his growth is challenged to his fullest potential. The individual's contribution and the validity of his feelings are of utmost importance. *In this way, the attitude of HEC is (ideally) in direct opposition to the general attitudes of society.*

*Children and Youth* (Englewood Cliffs: Prentice-Hall, 1971). p. 16.

2  *Ibid.*, pp. 87-88.

3  *Ibid,*. pp. 31-34.

Perhaps the most devastating attitude of society in general and churches in particular, is one of gentle patronization, clothed in a facade of deep concern for the welfare of the physically disabled individual. Programs, workshops, separate recreation programs, special enrichment programs, and crusades can exploit the fragile self image of even the strongest disabled person so poignantly that any help the program set out to provide is nullified.

"Except for psychiatric cases, the following generalizations seem reasonable:

1. No variation in physique requires psychological maladjustment.

2. If an emotional handicap exists in a person who has a physical disability, it does not stem directly from the disability but has been mediated by social variables.

3. The mediation between physical status and psychological behavior occurs in the following way:
   (a) The person lacks a tool that is required for behavior in the culture in which he lives, and he knows that he lacks it.
   (b) Other individuals perceive his lack and devaluate him for this reason.
   (c) The person accepts the judgment of others that he is less worthy (or to the degree that he is a product of his own culture, he judges himself less worthy) and devaluates himself."[4]

---

4 *Ibid.,* p. 14.

Within the structure of organized churches (as well as within the structure of society in general), there persists attitudes bordering on actual emotional deprivation for the physically disabled. The Apostolate of Misery and the American Society for Sick Catholics are religious organizations which seem, by their stated beliefs, to encourage physically disabled to be complacent, offer prayer for the world and silently bear their affliction.

Money is allocated from religious organizations such as the Knights of Columbus to provide transportation expenses for pilgrimages to various shrines and to Lourdes, France in hopes of miraculous cures. Belief in cures or other miracles is not the point of discussion here; rather that programs offered by churches and efforts made "on behalf of the disabled" *perpetuate the same values held by society*—that being physically disabled is to be less than a whole person.

If one can be "cured", one can then be whole. It is important to note that in the Gospels' accounts of Christ's healings, at no time does Christ indicate that the specific disability has been impairing the wholeness of the individual, rather he indicates that sins (perhaps what might be called in psychological terms, inner handicaps) are forgiven. Only then are those men made whole again.

A seemingly poor assumption has been drawn from Christ's use of the word "sin" while involved in the healing process. There still remains elements of Christianity that equate physical disability with sin. At a 1975 Conference of Catholic Educators of the Handicapped, Atlantic City, N.J. the assumption was drawn that disabilities are present in the world because sin is present in the world.

This attitude seems antiquated and out of touch with modern functional theory in the field of Sociology of Religion,[5] in which the scientific approach to society and religion coupled with knowledge of psychological development negates the "group mind" concepts prevalent in the last century.

It would appear that many attempts which are available to help the disabled individual, no matter how well meaning, fall far short of really providing him with the acceptance and contribution he finds necessary to be part of society and to consider himself as a whole individual.

## ATTITUDES OF THE HANDICAPPED TOWARD SELF

One of the obvious needs (perhaps the most obvious) of the handicapped individual is the need to provide for him an atmosphere and experiences which nurture positive self image. Striving for recognition of his basic good in some degree is crucial, because of the negative feelings about self held by the majority of disabled people. These often destructive feelings can be at the heart of non-actualizing living, infantile human relationships, a distant

---

5 Thomas F. O'Dea, *The Sociology of Religion* (Englewood Cliffs: Prentice-Hall, 1966), Chapter 1.

relationship with God, and a non-existent commitment to service to anyone but self.6

Changing these dehumanizing attitudes seems a definite part of the Gospel message to love one's fellow man, which hopefully is the reality of a Christian experience.

Physically disabled people have not all been disabled since birth. Those who have lived with disability since birth and/or early childhood have had years to grow in a particular life style. Therefore, if a person's self concept is poor partially as a result of society's reaction and his own reaction to his disability, he has had many years of reinforcement and is resistive to change.

If, however, an individual becomes disabled later in life, he has not had the lengthy negative reinforcement. But, any profound physical change can affect even the most positive attitudes. In working with individuals, those disabled since birth, and those recently disabled, common self-attitudes appear.

An individual's attitude about himself results largely from his family's attitude toward him, as well as general social attitudes.7 Since a disabled person often spends more years living with parents or relatives than do non-disabled people, the family attitude has great impact on self image. Society's radical view of wholeness and disability discussed

---

6 Samuel A. Kirk, *Educating Exceptional Children* (New York: Haughton Mifflin Company, 1972), Chapter 5.
7 Cruickshank, *op. cit.*, p. 14.

above, adds little to the hopes for positive self image from outside the family.

When a disabled child is born into a family, or becomes disabled in childhood, the child often becomes the center of family attention. This is due in part to guilt feelings of parents, and in part by the demand for time and energy of the family to provide for disabled person's physical needs. Frequently, an all-consuming absorption in self interest results which does not change as the person ages. A lack of stimulation is common in non-disabled people as well, but continuing dependence for basic survival needs tend to intensify self centeredness for the disabled.

Often, coupled with an inordinate self interest, are strong feelings of inferiority. Disabled people frequently come to believe that difference is not acceptable, not encouraged, and not respected.

The two above mentioned qualities—self centeredness and inferiority feelings, may seem unrelated, but actually feed each other, and at their base cause great internal pain and pose questions of loveability.

The disabled individual can believe that his family cares for him out of a sense of obligation, a feeling of guilt, or to expiate for some "sin". If these feelings are present, then to recognize that one will not be able to succeed by accepted standards may produce deep-seated doubts about personal worth.

In society's lifestyles one of the great measurements of self worth is accomplishment. The disabled person can rarely achieve in this milieu. Ergo, a reinforced feeling of worthlessness and poor self image.

When people do not believe in their intrinsic value, their lovableness, it becomes difficult to reach out in friendship. One then accepts being the receiver of friendship. If others take the time and exert the effort to recognize my worth, I may either disbelieve them and reject their efforts, or simply continue to be a recipient without the outward reaching needed for mutual positive regard.

So, the individual who so desperately needs the growth opportunities of friendship, frequently in effect resists them. Security is preferred to the risk of human relationships which may demand less self-centeredness, and challenge the disabled individual to believe his own lovability and self worth.

Another quality often present among the disabled is a great capacity for passivity. Even though a person can be self centered and demanding about his basic care needs, he can be oblivious to his obligation to take control of his own life. Often he exists at the whim and fancy of what others feel is good for him, or important to his life. It seems all too easy for the disabled individual to allow this to happen. He is easily manipulated by others' approval, though what he is expected to do may be in exact opposition to what the disabled person really wants.

It seems obvious then that the self worth of the disabled is easily questioned and that the process of "normal" self image development among the disabled is damaging to his personal self actualization and acceptance.

## GOALS OF HEC

The main thrust of HEC is to provide an atmosphere and experiences which can nurture spiritual growth for each person who attends and willingly participates to his fullest in the challenge of the weekend. HEC deals with basic Christian beliefs which challenge man to realize his full human potential in loving God, self and fellow man. This theology is not of any particular Christian denomination. It is the theology which attempts to bring deeper gospel meaning to every phase of each person's life.

HEC *is not*

>Doing good for poor unfortunates,
>Bearing a cross,
>Pitying self,
>Manipulating people,
>Comparing degrees of disability.

HEC *is*

>Songs and celebrations,
>Stillness and quiet,
>Dance and sharing,
>Giving and praying.

The belief that the Christian message must be presented in a dynamic, personal way leads HEC to establish the following goals.

First and foremost is to share the good news of Christ risen. Through committing experience, participation, and receiving information, those participants can reflect on their own lives, therein seeing the dying/new life/participation they share with

Christ Jesus. This core goal then, nurtures secondary goals which are self-explanatory.

1. To increase the handicapped individual's awareness of self worth.

2. To establish a positive identification for disabled people with a larger non-disabled community which the handicapped heretofore, have had little opportunity to establish on their own.

3. To increase communication between the disabled and non-disabled communities.

4. To normalize a weekend experience as much as possible for physically disabled people.

5. To encourage the handicapped person toward more independence and sociability.

6. To give those handicapped confined to institutions some time away from an institutional environment, and provide for them a time of loving care frequently not provided in the institutional setting.

7. To offer an opportunity for parents and/or relatives of handicapped persons to have some time away from the responsibility of caring for the physical needs of their son, daughter, or relative.

One of the above mentioned goals implies that the non-disabled will care for the physical needs of the handicapped during the weekend. These goals are offered to any disabled or non-disabled person who honestly wishes to participate in the HEC experience.

By adequate team preparation not only the care for physical needs is discussed, but the emotional and psychological needs of the disabled are discussed in some detail by a team member trained in behavioral science.

> ". . . when you have a party, invite the poor, the crippled, the lame, the blind; that they cannot pay you back means that you are fortunate, because repayment will be made to you when the virtuous rise again."[8]

Hopefully, by their joyful participation, HEC shall help each person respond in deeper unison in faith.

HEC exists because society does not believe that every man is equal to his brother, every woman to her sister.

HEC happens because society labels individuals as "handicapped." Such labels dehumanize.

HEC begins over and over so that blind folk, those in wheelchairs and folks with tottering steps, see themselves as valuable humans with great gifts to give the world.

HEC becomes a needed experience wherein man meets himself, recognizes his beauty and acknowledges his disabilities.

HEC recurs so that man can find and nurture his friendship with God.

## THEMES OF THE HEC WEEKEND

The basic theme of HEC is the dying, rising, going forth which threads through the Christian

---

8 "The Gospel of Luke," 14:13-14, *Good News for Modern Man* (New York: American Bible Society, 1971), p. 191.

experience. In other words, the Paschal Mystery is central to this HEC experience. The Paschal Mystery holds a key place in the weekend as it does in the TEC weekend experience.

Because of its centrality the entire weekend is designed around the paschal mystery theme. Friday evening is set aside for familiarization with self and others, as well as generally getting acquainted.

*Saturday* is a day spent in deeper study of one's relation to God, and in finding those inner parts we wish to discard and die to. The *Sunday* theme is that of new, changed life.

*Monday's* emphasis is directed toward beginning a changed life and re-entering the everyday world with the Good News that has been discovered during this weekend.

Part of the entire weekend experience is to challenge and explore one's self, one's thoughts, attitudes and one's individual relationship with God as it is related to the Paschal Mystery and to each individual's life. Self exploration is related directly to the basic Paschal Mystery theme.

As part of encountering self, others, and God, the issue of being handicapped is confronted directly and discussed openly and honestly.

The entire weekend experience enables all participants to identify and become part of a Gospel Christian community.

The group of believers was one in mind and heart. No one said that any of his belongings was his own, but they all shared with one another everything they had. With great power the apostles gave witness to the resurrection of the Lord Jesus, and God poured rich blessings on them all. There was no one in the group who was in need. Those who owned fields or houses would sell them, bring the money received from the sale and turn it over to the apostles; and the money was distributed to each one according to his need.[9]

## PREPARATION FOR THE WEEKEND

Preparation for the HEC weekend is perhaps as important as the weekend itself. Actual team preparation and selection, selection of adequate facilities, and the ever-present need for fund-raising are discussed in some detail in this chapter. Each aspect of the process necessary for preparation for the HEC experience is vitally important to the success of the experience. It is obvious that great amounts of time and energy are expended in preparation for each weekend experience. Some idea of what is necessary in preparation is discussed below.

### TEAM PREPARATION

Prior to every HEC a large team is selected. Besides the need for table leaders and speakers, there is need for people who will provide one to one care for the more severely physically disabled people, to help with dressing, eating, etc. This necessitates a large team which also allows for more involvement for nondisabled people.

Within the team, members manifest different

9 Acts 4:32-35 (*Good News for Modern Man*).

strengths. Some are excellent table leaders, others are stimulating speakers. There are some who relate well on a one to one basis but would not do well in the leadership or speaker role. Because of its design HEC gives these people an opportunity for vital involvement which they might not have on other retreat teams.

The *team members* come from varied backgrounds. They are blue collar workers, professional people, students, lay people, religious, and clergy. They are selected on the basis of their Christian life-style. That is, they are selected because of active Gospel involvement, not how eloquently they speak of it. This screening process is carried out because of deep belief that the principle impressions of a weekend are experiences of honest community and Gospel loving, not remembering the content of long speeches.

The following characteristics come closest to describing qualities desired in team members: flexibility, sensitivity to self and others, nonpatronizing attitude toward the handicapped, a keen sense of humor, and an ability to laugh at self, avoidance of a verbally overpowering "used car salesmanship" approach to Christianity, an easy ability, as team member, to divorce oneself from self's needs, and lastly, the capability of not taking one's role as a team member too seriously.

The actual direction of the weekend and team meetings which is shared by three people, one of whom assumes final responsibility, must blend in harmony through the cooperation of these key individuals. During the team meetings and the weekend itself, the directors function to act as time keepers, to assess the continuity and flow of the weekend, to serve as sounding boards for concerns which arise, and to interact with the retreat house staff about any business concerns.

Because of liturgical celebrations on the weekend it is necessary to have *at least one priest* as part of the team. His commitment to HEC and its follow-up activities is very important. Not only is this crucial, but this minister must be a self-actualizing person possessing not only the desired qualities indicated for team members above, but also a deep-seeded faith commitment to Gospel living and service.

An understanding of and ability to celebrate meaningful theologically sound ritual must also be his contribution. Because each of the above mentioned qualities is so vital, not every priest is well suited to HEC involvement.

Another important member of the team is the *music director* who must be versed in playing an appropriate instrument, possibly a guitar. This musician must be sensitive to the mood of the moment, have a large repertoire of songs to fit the unexpected needs for song, as well as the scheduled times. An ability to work closely and tirelessly with the directors makes the music director's position a very sensitive one.

There is great need, too, for a *responsible individual to plan and direct serving of all meals*. The cook not only plans the meals but recruits a group of volunteers to assist in preparing and serving meals and snacks as well as any needed special diets.

Purchasing and soliciting donations of food are the co-responsibilities of both director and cook. The latter must also direct maintaining the dining area throughout the weekend and simultaneously see that the staff is integrated into the entire HEC experience.

As adjunct to the team, there is a core of volunteers who do not function on the weekend itself, but arrange and provide transportation to and from the retreat center. Public transportation is purposely avoided. Integrating lives in providing transportation forces personal contact between disabled and nondisabled.

This is often the beginning step for those nondisabled who previously feared being with disabled people. It may also be the beginning of a HEC involvement for those who are not ready yet for a weekend commitment. This method of transportation becomes a visible sign to the disabled that many people care about their well-being. The transportation volunteer group becomes part of a total fifty to sixty people fortunate enough to share in each HEC.

To the people involved are given the following responsibilities:

1. To be alert and sensitive to the general feeling of the group. If for example, HECers are restless, to suggest to the directors the need for singing or for a change of activity.

2. To be assigned to a particular individual and to a table group, and to try to get to know as many of the HECers as possible in that group.

3. To be very conscious of the uniqueness and

great potential waiting inside each person on the retreat.

4. To be aware that there is no team-candidate differentiation on a HEC weekend.

5. To take time at meals and at breaks to get to know everyone on the weekend as well as possible—each has a great deal to offer.

6. To be aware that team members are not a fearless leader or fountain of Christian advice. Questions put to team members by those expecting profound immediate advice, should be thrown back to the questioner.

7. On Friday evening at the tables the team is asked to be primarily listeners since as the weekend unfolds each person is encouraged to participate and formulate his or her own ideas.

8. To try to emphasize individual goodness and beauty.

9. To try to have the discussions of talks relate to real life situations.

10. At each table to try to build the idea of a small community.

11. Be an example. Be excited about participation in discussions and reactions.

12. To watch for cliques. Do not break them up, just broaden them by joining.

13. HEC does not try to tire participants, but somehow bedtime is seldom before midnight. As a responsible person, it is important to encourage adequate rest.

14. To trust, be full of faith, and be full of love,

while not judging the progress of the weekend or of any individual.

15. If there are problems or questions, resolve them as quickly as possible.

16. Participate, don't anticipate.

17. To enjoy the celebration spirit of the weekend and the celebration that God and man, and man and God together can cause.

Prior to each HEC weekend, a series of four or five team meetings is held with as many team members as possible present. The meetings are held once a week for the month prior to the HEC.

The *first meeting* concentrates on three general areas. There is general getting acquainted with each other along with an attempt to know each other in some depth.

Also, an introduction and explanation of the goals and general schedule of the weekend is presented. Lastly, the directors explain the themes of the weekend and ideas for the talks, then ask specific team members to prepare a specific talk, but giving them the option to refuse.

The *second meeting* involves getting the team better acquainted and with the use of Scripture exercises, hopefully, begins to build a Christ-centered community. People are given time to share their ideas about talks, clarify any confusions, and elicit ideas from the total team for a particular talk.

Lastly, each person participates in some exercises which delve into people's attitudes toward the whole idea of handicaps. These are the crucial items of the second meeting. However, some time is also given to beginning work in fund raising.

*Meeting number three* has more exercises geared to getting to know more deeply one's self, others and one's relationship with God. Part of this knowing self more deeply is to discover one's own handicaps. This, plus a discussion of the team's role, constitute much of the meeting. It is important at this meeting, however, that the group worship together as part of their beginning to live a Christian community.

The *last meeting* begins with a work session, getting together the necessary details. Directors acquaint the team with the candidates by means of their applications and accompanying letters. At this meeting there should be time for quiet to pray alone and with others, and there should be time to share fears, questions, comments, all that has brought people together up to this point. Then worship together.


## THE FORMAT OF THE WEEKEND


In order to better understand the progression and format of the HEC weekend, two schedules used on recent retreat weekends will be discussed in detail. It is important to note that in keeping with the general themes of the weekend, the specific schedule need not be rigidly exacting. There is nothing magic in the sequence of events, just as there is no exact way to experience God.

The HEC weekend generally lasts for three and one half days. The particular weekends which will be described here lasted from Friday evening through Monday afternoon. The HEC weekend is divided into four major themes, each one having a period of time within the schedule devoted to that theme. The underlying theme of the weekend, as explained previously, is the paschal mystery theme of life, through death, to changed life.

On Friday evening at a designated time and retreat center, those who will participate gather together. An exact schedule with explanation follows:

*FRIDAY:*

*General Theme: Encountering and Discovery*

7:30 *Arrival of Candidates*

> The retreatants (candidates) arrive from a wide geographic area and are transported by volunteer helpers. The arrival times vary, due to difficulty in transporting needed equipment (wheelchairs, etc.) and great traveling distances.

> *Music and Snacks*

> For many of those arriving it has been a long trip to unfamiliar areas with unfamiliar people. Availability of snacks and music plays an important part in making strangers comfortable with one another and providing a homelike atmosphere.

8:15 *Opening Prayer*

> This prayer begins the weekend and asks God's blessings on our mutual endeavor. It is simply stated and avoids lengthy rhetoric.

## 8:20 *Orientation Talk*

A short orientation talk explains the mood of the weekend and tries to calm any fears. Freedom to participate or not to participate in any part of the weekend is stressed. Facilities for sleeping, bathrooming, and medical assistance, etc., are explained, and the challenge is offered to leave the retreat on Monday as a changed person.

As a reaction to this talk, table groups are assigned and some time is spent in getting acquainted with those in this table group. Then a name for the table is chosen by common consent. This establishes some immediate identity with a small group within the retreat weekend group.

From then on when speaking to the larger group, each person is asked to introduce himself with his name and his table's name. Others at the tables are encouraged to show obvious support by loud applause for this person's willingness to contribute. After the tables have been named, and some graphic display of the name rendered, one or two table members explain to the larger group what the name means and how that name was chosen.

## 9:00 *Ideals of Adulthood Talk*

This is a short talk designed to begin discussion within the table groups. It is not a God-oriented talk. This talk explores the process of choosing ideals and goals and reaching them. It defines ideals.

Emphasis is placed on the need for goals and ideals to be self-determined rather than other-determined. It also discusses the continuing change in goals and ideals, and finally challenges each participant to form some of his or her own ideals.

As a reaction to the Ideals Talk, each table is asked to discuss the ideas they have just heard and to not simply re-hash what the speaker stated, but allow their discussion to follow its own course in the general area of ideals.

One person is chosen or volunteers to act as a secretary and later share the table group's ideas with the larger group. A poster incorporating the ideas discussed is also used, and this affords an opportunity for another table member to express ideas by explaining the poster.

10:00 *Encountering Self and Others Talk*

This talk incorporates ideas about falseness, honesty with self, the multiplicity of selves within one person, various facets of personality (e.g. emotions, intelligence, etc.) and challenges participants toward acceptance and identification of strengths and weaknesses. Emphasis is placed in discovering a person's strengths. The talk also explores the need for change within oneself.

Being part of a group and one's interaction with others is also discussed. The need to approach encountering others and self, to work at this, and not let encounter be wholly controlled by glands are stressed ideas in this particular talk.

As a reaction, each participant is given a piece of clay and asked to fashion a symbol as an image of himself, and then place his image in relationship to each person at the table. The clay symbols are displayed throughout the weekend so that they can be shared with all participants.

11:00 *Meditation on Love of Life*

As a closing for the evening, a short meditation on the sacredness of life and the unity of man with all living things is presented. A challenge and need to share and choose life are also stressed.

11:10 *Snack and Bed*

Perhaps one of the most important aspects of the HEC weekend experience especially for the nondisabled, is the actual physical care needed by the more severely disabled.

Relationships are quickly formed on a need basis, but friendship frequently is forthcoming. The actual physical needs, and the desire to communicate these needs, breaks down polite social taboos and enables both parties to enter into more real and meaningful communication.

## SATURDAY:

*General Theme: Discovery of the Need to Change
and a*
## CHALLENGE TO BE DIFFERENT

### 7:30 *Arise*

Naturally it is necessary that the participants involved in physical care arise prior to this time. It is stressed that extreme care be taken for a disabled person's feelings of privacy and modesty, and that hygiene be not neglected for those unable to care for their own needs. The attitude is one of cheerfulness and excitement in facing a new day.

### 8:15 *Meditation on Discovery*

For this meditation the entire group gathers in a designated area, perhaps the chapel, to hear some brief thoughts on the need for each of us to broaden our horizons. The idea is pointed out that man by his nature is driven to go beyond himself and to discover beautiful things in himself and in those around him. Mutual willingness to risk discovery is hoped for.

### 8:20 *Breakfast*

Meal time is a time for socialization as well as nourishment. Table groups do not remain together and it is important that everyone tries to get to know everyone else. This breakfast is also the first time that some of the participants will be able to meet the kitchen staff.

Problems with feeding are handled by anyone who is able to help. Good humor and cheerfulness are encouraged. After breakfast a time for telling jokes and short humorous stories adds to the general relaxed quality of the meal.

9:30 *Encountering God Talk*

The encountering God talk is broken into two basic parts. The first part concentrates on God's reaching out, ever willing to be involved with man, with man's choice to encounter a loving God, the instances of God reaching and man encountering God as found in Scripture, and the uniqueness of God-man encounters.

The second part of the talk deals with how we encounter God, via people, words, music, nature, etc., introduces the Word of God (New Testaments), and expresses man's desire to hear God and encounter Him. This is the first talk of the weekend that directly labels man's search for God, and invites us all to participate.

As a reaction to this talk each participant is given a New Testament for his own, furnished by the American Bible Society. Time is allowed for silent reading, then sharing passages and using the New Testaments. This is encouraged at the tables and with the whole group.

It is important that braille copies of the Bible are furnished for blind participants as well as large print editions for those with gross and fine motor control problems so to enable them to read more easily.

10:30 *The Paschal Mystery Talk*

The Paschal Mystery talk deals with the core experience of Christianity and is central to this weekend. The approach to the Paschal Mystery is generally the "death to new life" approach common during Lenten liturgies.

The emphasis is that as a community in the next few days, people will journey through a look at self, a weeding-out process of that which they do not like, a putting away of old useless things, shedding these "grave clothes", and then coming to a new life which will be controlled by self with the help of God and others.

The summary and poster reaction explained above is once again used. Table ideas are shared with the entire group.

11:30 *Break*

At this time all participants are urged to take a recreational break, walk around, see the grounds, or just engage in quiet conversation. This enables people not already acquainted to establish some relationship.

12:30 *Lunch*

See the explanation for breakfast.

## 1:30 *On Being Handicapped Talk*

This talk, as well as the Paschal Mystery talk, is central to the weekend experience. Information is discussed regarding the social implications of handicapping. It is emphasized that each person is handicapped in some way. Wholeness is discussed. What one does with obvious difference, how one approaches the world with recognized handicaps, and the hopefulness involved in recognition of handicaps as well as strengths are the central themes.

Control of one's destiny regardless of physical disability is also discussed. This talk must be given by a team member with great credibility among the disabled community. Honest feelings must be discussed sincerely and frankly. Since this is the first talk that deals directly with the problems facing disabled, it naturally can set the mood of honesty and reality for the remainder of the weekend.

Reaction to the Handicapped talk usually assumes the form of table discussions, then a general discussion with no specific reports from the previous table discussions. Often there is a lengthy question and answer period during which questions of sexuality, worth as a human being, and other topics are discussed.

## 3:15 *Metanoia Talk*

The metanoia talk is primarily a witness talk. The term metanoia, meaning a complete turning about, is explained using the references to St. Paul's conversion. The idea of a complete change of heart (not merely a surface change), a long lasting change with a recognizable difference in life style as a result of a recognition of the need for change, is the major thrust of the speaker.

The speaker's own change of heart is discussed with an honest discussion of motives and actions centering around that change. The challenge for all present to risk taking a chance and to be open to change is re-emphasized. The reaction to this talk is simply done in a graphic poster and shared by an explanation of that poster. The posters, as in the past, are displayed throughout the meeting room for later inspection.

4:15 *Penance Talk*

The penance talk is a talk about reconciliation, joining together what had been separated. It is not an attempt to promote deep guilt feelings for offending God and fellowman. The option is rather coming to one's senses as did the prodigal son, and making a conscious choice for goodness, in other words, putting aside that which keeps one from being all that he can be.

The joy of reconciliation is explored as is the need to be reconciled with one another. This talk should be approached simply and with little pedagogy.

A paraliturgical celebration is the reaction

to this talk. Each participant willing to do so is asked to write on a piece of paper those inner things which he would like to rid himself of and for which he willingly seeks forgiveness. The papers are then collected and ritually burned.

The flame from this fire is used to enkindle a new light of the Paschal Candle which burns continuously throughout the remainder of the weekend and follows the entire group to meals, the chapel, etc., as a reminder of their promises. This paraliturgical service is generally done in quiet, but singing may accompany the service.

5:15 *Private Confession or Break*

During this time period those wishing to receive the sacrament of reconciliation are free to do so; priests are available for private confession. Others may wish simply to rest, walk about the grounds or share in small discussion groups.

6:00 *Dinner*

This major meal of the day is generally joyful after the seriousness of the paraliturgy.

7:15 *Signs Talk*

The signs talk stresses man's need for symbolism and emphasizes communication. Symbol becomes sign when it takes a special personal meaning of itself. It is possible that this weekend may become a sign, together, and individually. Examples of symbols and

*The problem of public financial aid, architectural barriers, or the legal rights of deviant individuals are secondary concerns within the framework of HEC's goal which is that the disabled person should be accepted, respected and considered as a whole person and be given an environment in which his growth is challenged to its fullest potential.*

signs of the weekend are explained in some detail.

Reaction to this talk takes the form of sign. Cornstarch and water are mixed; participants experiment with the peculiar properties of this mixture. Each person is then asked to express his sign value from the cornstarch. Discussion of the various sign values follows. One of the signs emphasized in the signs talk is the sign of the Passover and Last Supper which the Church retains in the form of the Mass.

8:15 *Liturgy* (Mass)

A liturgy planned to emphasize the reconciliation qualities of signs is shared by willing participants. (No one is forced to take part in any of the weekend activities.) A foot-washing service is included, with each participant given the opportunity to wash the feet of others present, as a sign of service and love.

Baptismal promises are either renewed or individually written and shared, and a service of stoles (a white garment traditionally given at Baptism), is offered to each participant. The liturgical celebration is one of great joy because, symbolically, new life has begun for each participant.

10:15 *Palanca*

Palanca is a Spanish word literally meaning "lever." This is explained to the group. While the retreatants have been spending time on this weekend together, other Christians have been praying for their successful encounter with Christ. These prayers come in many forms and are offered as a way of pushing down on one end of the "lever" in order to lift up the other end (participants).

Written expressions of the larger Christian community's concerns and hopes for the weekend are addressed and given to each participant. The general effect of this support helps each participant understand that there is a larger community who will support them and who care for them even though they are not physically present. Palanca is then shared with other participants.

10:45 *Meditation on Forgiveness*

This short meditation emphasizes the joy of the forgiveness process, the feeling of unity and wholeness and the excitement of new beginning.

11:00 *Snack and Bed*


*SUNDAY:*


*General Theme: Celebration of New, Changed Life—Celebration of Community*

7:30 *Rise*

8:15 *Meditation of the Risen Christ*

This meditation with the entire group centers

238

on the coming of new life by recalling Christ's resurrection into a changed form of life. Participants are asked to put yesterday away and now begin a new life. The joy of new life and the excitement of being alive are major themes.

9:30 *God, A Community of Life and Love Talk*

This talk presents a look at God through "new" eyes. God as a concept of childhood (as Santa or Warden), is replaced by the concept of a vital and alive God. The need for one another is presented through the illustration of the Trinity whose principle work is to promote being—or love. A challenge is presented in the form of God calling all to new life together as a community.

As a reaction to this talk each table group is asked to form some symbol, using themselves to express life and love as a community. These symbols are then shared with the entire group.

10:30 *Christian Life Talk*

The Christian life talk discusses the meaning of being involved in a new life in Christ. It emphasizes that the call to new life must be uniquely individual and that it is a call to love, which can only be an individual response. Being open to all, new and old, and the need for vulnerability are also stressed.

The individual's function within the community is discussed. Some personal experience of response, and the results of living a new life, may also be appropriate. As one way of remaining open to the call for new life, prayer is introduced, alone and together.

At this time the concept of prayer as a recited formula can be clarified, that is, prayer is a response to a call from God; spontaneous prayer is encouraged. As a response to this talk table groups are invited to share prayer with each other at some quiet place.

11:30 *Break*

12:00 *Lunch*

1:30 *People of God Talk*

This talk stresses the commonality of all mankind. The people of God are those who have freely chosen to become aware and respond to the call to newness. Yet, one must always question who is calling. Is it personal motivation or does motivation come from God?

It is noted that there is a great variety of calls from God. All men who have an awareness of changed life respond in some way to that call. The call from God to new life encompasses Jews, Buddhists, Islams and Christians of other persuasions. The important recognition is that God is calling and reaching. Man must choose to respond in his own cultural and individual way.

The summary and poster reaction is used with this talk.

2:20 *Church in the World Talk*

Certain belief is that Christ changed the world in fact and in spirit. All men have a new, special invitation to life. Those who heed this invitation and call are the Church. The Church is not an organization but, rather, a way of life.

The next obvious question is what the Church is challenged to do in this world. The response is to do things that are rather foolish; love enemies, return good for evil, hope for truth even when it hurts, etc. Discussion of the difference between selfish motives and true "Church" motives would also be emphasized. The Gospel call to be a fool for Christ and the command to love are emphasized, as well as the need to recognize the necessary, vital support from others.

Reaction to the Church in the world talk takes form in a clown reaction with one or more people participating. The content of this reaction stems from the weekend dynamic at this time. Discussions and questions arising from the weekend itself should be dealt with in a humorous way. As with much of the weekend itself, description without experience leaves a void for the reader.

3:15 *Break*

4:00 *Liturgy*

This liturgical celebration emphasizes the role of community in the journey of the people of God. The small community formed here for the weekend, the community of family, and the larger community of mankind, are blended into one with the emphasis placed on the brotherhood of all and the equality of each individual within the group.

5:15 *Dinner*

6:30 *Hootenanny*

The hootenanny is a songfest celebration of community to which many of the Christian community come. There are songs and general exuberance at welcoming the retreatants into the larger community. This gathering is a visible symbol to the participants that the community which has been discussed during the day is a viable, real community.

Parents of younger participants, and friends of all are especially invited to show their approval for the choice to a changed life. A general party atmosphere prevails with refreshments and singing and, occasionally limited amounts of dancing.

At a point during the festivities, all are asked to be seated and each retreat participant is introduced individually to the community. Anyone who wishes may speak about his experience. The table names are given and explained by a table member. If a raffle has been used to raise money for support of the weekend, winners are chosen at this time.

Then, a more serious note is injected into the festivities; a talk is given on the subject of Christian peace.

The speaker alternates with the singers, giving comments on the verses of the Peace Song. Since there is such variety of response to song, each speaker's talk has a special flavor of its own. At the end of the hootenanny, some form of total community affirmation in song or prayer (generally in a circle with hands held), sends the visitors home and is the signal for the retreat to continue.

8.30 *Skits*

Just for fun, and because physically disabled individuals seldom have the opportunity to indulge in group make-believe, some time is set aside for the planning and execution of skits. The skits have little or nothing to do with the weekend other than providing a time for all to be fools and to perform and entertain one another.

Costumes, makeup, and properties are provided. After a time of preparation, the amateur theatrical productions unfold for the whole group. The expression of joy is contagious and most participants in the retreat willingly don outrageous costumes and happily make fools of themselves for one another.

10:30 *Shared Palanca*

At the hootenanny much more palanca has been brought in by the community. A time is set aside to share that palanca, and to share thoughts that the participants may be having about the weekend. This offers each person the opportunity to express himself

243

in front of a large group of accepting, loving individuals. For some participants, this sharing is the first time they have ever been able to speak in front of a group.

11:00 *Meditation on Love*

This short meditation expresses the need to love and be loved, and the need to work at loving, not just hoping that love happens. Individuals are encouraged to express openly their love for one another and for this group.

*MONDAY:*

*General Theme: Living a New Life Among Old Things*

7.30 *Rise*

8:20 *Meditation on Confidence in Christ*

This meditation is presented with the whole group. It stresses the need to get comfortable with one's new found life, as well as introduces the obligation to reach out to others and share what has been found. This reaching out process cannot be preachy or condescending, but must reflect a genuine regard for others' lives and their choice to live them as they choose. The challenge is to be changed and to be open to further change while not being fearful to be different.

8:30 *Breakfast*

## 9:30 *Life-styles Talk*

The speaker for the Life-styles talk is obliged, first of all, to make the talk appropriate to the participants. This talk is a frank discussion of various life style alternatives, those things that limit or mold life-style choice. The emphasis is on choice, rather than circumstance, and how one changes over and over again.

The myth that occupations determine life-style is discussed. The Christian life-style—the choice to live for others, is discussed at some length. Discussion is stimulated, and a challenge to choose a Christian life-style is presented.

Reaction to this talk is a general open discussion in which alternatives available for disabled are discussed. Problems are seldom solved but possible ideas as to how one might change an institutional setting, or an overprotective family, are discussed.

## 11:30 *Break for Packing*

This time is spent in gathering all belongings to be put back into the luggage and made ready for the transportation volunteers to take participants back to their homes. All belongings wanted—posters, Bibles, clay images, etc., are carefully packed for the homeward trip.

## 12:30 *Lunch*

## 1:45 *Christianity in Action Talk*

The Christianity in Action talk explores the possibilities of each participant's involvement in the Christian community. Avenues of available work such as telephone hot lines, visits to hospitals, involvement in Church related activities, and family communications may be stressed.

The emphasis is on unique contributions of the individual. Causes are not stressed, but genuine, honest involvement with others is emphasized. Those who can write are encouraged to send letters to inmates in prisons, or to write palanca for others making similar weekends. The similarities of the terms Christianity and Action, seem foremost in planning for this talk.

Reaction to the talk is to use fingerpaints to express Christian involvement and action. (Fingerpainting is another activity in which few disabled people have been able to participate.)

2:45 *Beyond HEC Talk*

To the whole group (tables are pushed aside at this point in the weekend), the speaker addresses himself to a "safe togetherness" here on the weekend, where people attempt to live a Gospel Christian community, and the need to leave the retreat changed in some way. Reactions to this changed life which people might encounter are also discussed.

The reality that all will need one another's support is also stressed. For that support each participant is reminded that there are periodic reunions, news letters, small get togethers, etc., that need each person. Although people separate physically, there is a common bond that draws them together if they have recognized the call to change during this weekend.

Anyone wishing to share further thoughts regarding the weekend is encouraged to do so. The need for all to be joyful together, even in parting, is encouraged.

3:30 *Final Liturgy and Commissioning Service*

The final Liturgy is again one of joy. It does not ignore what people have experienced together, but it also does not dwell on sadness at leaving one another. As a part of the final Liturgy a commissioning service takes place.

During this service each participant is called to the front of the community and given a list of addresses, telephone numbers, and birthdays of all present. A cross with the inscription, "Christ is counting on You", is presented to each participant and also a certificate suitable for framing is presented as a gentle reminder of the challenge of the weekend.

A blessing is given to each individual by laying-on of hands in ancient Christian tradition. After the final service the weekend is at an end.

# ALTERNATE SCHEDULE

## FRIDAY

### General Theme: Discovering Feelings

**8:30 Welcome**

One of the leaders of the weekend begins the weekend and offers a word of welcome.

**8:40 Opening Prayer**

(See previous schedule)

**8:45 Orientation Talk**

(See previous schedule)

As a reaction to this talk, the participants are encouraged to jot ideas in a journal provided for them. Specific time during the weekend will be provided to put additional thoughts in the journal.

**9:15 Introductions**

Informal introductions of individuals at the tables.

**9:35 Feelings Talk**

Ideas to be included in this talk are as follows: Getting in touch with feelings. We all have feelings. Feelings are neither good nor bad, they simply are. We sometimes avoid recognition of feelings. We are asked on this weekend to see our feelings and recognize them as they are. Can we live only by feelings? What are your feelings?

As a reaction to this talk, a life size doll is displayed in a prominent place and individuals are encouraged to speak out about their feelings right now and these feelings are written on the doll.

A question sheet is also provided regarding feelings and serves as a stimulus for table discussion.

10:45 *Table Naming*

(See previous schedule)

11:30 *Meditation on Looking into Self*


*SATURDAY:*


*Theme: Becoming Human*

7:30 *Rise*

8:15 *Meditation on Humanity*

8:30 *Breakfast*

9:15 *Transition Activity*

Feelings Cards—Each person is given five 3 x 5 cards on which he or she puts one word to describe feelings about self. Each card has a different feeling. The cards are then arranged in order of importance. The first two cards are discussed and each individual tells why he feels that way.

### 9:35 *Being Human Talk*

Ideas for this talk include: What does it mean to be human? What are the things that comprise us and make us human? It is good to be human. We are a complete part of the universe. It is not good to deny any part of our humanity. We feel, we think, we have fun, etc. We can become more fully human. This talk is not specifically about God.

As a reaction to this talk, each participant is asked to make a clay symbol to represent what it means to be human to him personally. The symbols are discussed at the tables.

### 10:45 *Being Handicapped Talk*

Ideas encompassed in this talk are: Being handicapped is part of our humanity. Discussion of society's labels. Differentiation between handicapped and disabled. Handicaps are common to all. How do we handicap ourselves?

Do we allow part of ourselves to become handicapped? What are psychological handicaps? Do our handicaps determine our perceptions in life? Can we overcome and do we need to overcome disabilities? We need to recognize disabilities realistically, acknowledge them and live around them.

Reaction to this talk is first in the small table groups and then in a large discussion.

**11:30** *Free Time*

**12:30** *Dinner*

**1:20** *Time for writing in Journals*

**1:30** *Humanity of Jesus Talk*

Ideas for the talk: Jesus was the human of humans. He said "yes" to life completely, what does this mean? He was completely human (examples from scriptures). Jesus felt and experienced the frustrations we feel. He is an example for us to enter completely into life with total trust in the Father. Jesus still lives and is human and that is good.

At this time the Paschal candle is lit indicating Jesus has the light. The candle lighting is followed by a bible paraliturgy in which one leader calls names individually, another leader reads aloud verses selected by participants. A third leader hands each participant a New Testament.

**2:30** *Change—A Human Challenge*

Ideas to be included: Change is an integral part of being human. Growth dictates change. Speaker stresses personal experiences of change—a real turning in life. Change is frightening and also very exciting. Change is a challenge.

As a reaction to this talk, a quiet time to think about change in your own life.

**3:00** *Penance and Reconciliation*

One of the priests present speaks briefly about

the sacrament of reconciliation. The Penance paraliturgy is the same as described in the previous schedule.

4:00 *Free Time*

5:30 *Dinner*

6:00  *Selfishness to Servanthood Talk*

Ideas to be stressed:  Selfishness is easy. Selfishness is part of what we think of as self-protection. Sometimes doing good things is selfishly rewarded. We frequently have the idea that we are the center of the universe. Our inability to accept differences in people is directly related to how self-centered we are.

Can selfishness be changed into usefulness or servanthood? What is real servanthood? How can we make the change from being selfish to being servants? How does God play a part in this change? Can we really love others as much as ourselves?

Reaction to this talk:  Two appropriate questions are posed to the group and each table answers among themselves. A poster is produced by each table which symbolizes the whole day so far and the posters are shared with the entire group.

8:00 *Liturgy*

Service of foot washing included.

9:15 *Palanca*

(See previous schedule)

10:10 *Write in journals*

10:30 *Meditation—Jesus in our lives*

*SUNDAY:*

    *Theme: Choosing Christianity*

7:30 *Rise*

8:15 *Meditation on Making Choices*

8:30 *Breakfast*

9:20 *Time to write in journals*

9:30 *Talk:  Man's Relationship with God*

Ideas stressed in this talk:  God has called throughout the ages. There is a mutual need between God and man. God loves us with perfect love. God is not Santa, etc. but a genuine lover of his people. God loves individually and as a group. What is an individual relationship with God?

The following questions are used for discussion with the tables:

1) Think of someone for whom God plays an important role in his life. What effect has it had on his life and on your life.

2) When were you first aware of God?

3) As you see it, how has God treated you in life?

4) What is your relationship with God?

A poster is also used to show common elements that run through individual relationships with God.

10:30 *Talk: Communication between God and Man*

A group of four people are given five minutes to talk about their prayer life.

As a reaction, everyone is asked to pray by table groups in a suitable place.

12:15 *Lunch*

1:00 *The Cost of Choosing Christianity Talk*

These elements should be included: Has Christianity really meant anything in life? Does the core meaning of Christianity demand any conscious decisions? Decisions to live a certain way invariably bring conflict. What does the choice mean personally?

How much will I do to live this Christianity? What does it say if my God relationship has never cost me anything? Is it inevitable that if Christianity is taken and lived seriously, one will be persecuted for it?

Reaction: Individuals are asked to answer the following questions and discuss them at the table:

1) Have you as yet consciously made a choice to live Christianity and explain it?

2) What has Christianity cost someone you know?

3) Has your Christianity ever cost you anything?

4) How far will you go in trying to live the gospel?

**2:00** *Christian Community Talk*

Ideas to be stressed: The meaning of community. What does Christian Community add to that meaning of community? The word Christian should not limit but expand to include. What does scripture say about Christian community? Share experiences about this type of community.

Reaction: Non-verbal group expression. Each table group, after some discussion expresses Christian community in a non-verbal symbol.

**3:45** *Liturgy*: Theme of Community is emphasized

**5:30** *Dinner*

**6:30** *Hootenanny*

(See previous schedule)

**9:30** *Skits*

(See previous schedule)

**11:30** *Meditation on Peace*

*MONDAY:*

*Theme: Going Forth*

**7:30** *Rise*

**8:15** *Meditation on the need to respond*

**8:30** *Breakfast*

9:20 *Write in Journals*

9:30 *Transition: Decisions and Risks*

Appropriate questions are formulated and asked to emphasize the need for making decisions and the risks involved in decision making.

10:00 *Beatitudes Talk*

Ideas to be stressed: Our relationship with God offers the greatest challenge in becoming fully human. God lures us more deeply into relationship with Him. With intimacy comes suffering—needed to grow. With the sorrow comes great joy. Jesus has already told us how to live and what to expect. What do the Beatitudes mean?

Reaction: Clown reaction (See previous schedule).

10:45 *Christian response in living Talk*

Ideas: The essence of the gospel is to love. Explore the meaning of Christian love. (Use St. Paul's first letter to the Corinthians) Love—the antidote to selfish demands, the ultimate. What is the meaning of jealousy? keeping records of wrongs? etc.

Reaction: Discussion with the entire group.

12:00 *Free Time*

12:30 *Dinner*

1:15 *Time set aside for writing palanca for other HECs*

**1:45** *Beginnings Talk*

> Ideas: A time to come to grips with the past and learn from it. Take the experience of the weekend and the gospel presentations of the weekend—What does it say to me as an individual? Meet the present moment then choose to decide. Begin a new way to live. Life simply is!

**2:15** *Write in journals*

**2:45** *Final Liturgy*

> (See previous schedule)

## FACILITIES

A number of facilities have been used for the HEC retreat weekends; no facility has been designed specifically for the needs of physically disabled. When the weekends first began, a no-longer-used dormitory building at the Mary Immaculate School in Ossining was used. This was a multi-leveled, multi-storied building which required ramps to be built for the use of wheelchairs. The bathroom facilities were difficult because of narrow doorways.

Another facility, Mt. Florence in Peekskill, New York, required extensive ramps built outdoors, up along flight of stairs, through a cloistered chapel and into a second floor sleeping area. Since that time five other facilities have been used; none has been ideal, yet the facility itself has made little difference to the dynamic of the weekend.

There are basic conditions necessary for the physical plant, yet as long as a majority of these are met, then minor problems can be overlooked.

One basic consideration is to have some sleeping rooms on the same floor as the meeting room so as to accommodate those in wheelchairs. The meeting room should be large and airy with ample room to accommodate about sixty people, of whom approximately twenty are in wheelchairs or stretcher carts. If this room is damp it causes unnecessary suffering for people with arthritis. Ideally, a separated dining room and chapel is helpful for change of scene, but this is not a necessity.

One other factor worth mentioning is that it is easier for the HEC weekend when a team member does the cooking and provides food services, since frequently special diets are needed, and changes are more readily and quickly facilitated with this type arrangement.

The single most important aspect of the facility for the weekend is the attitude and cooperation of those who operate the retreat house. Almost any inconvenience can be overcome if the attitude of the retreat house staff is flexible and enthusiastic.

The team can and does easily overcome architectural problems. Many times, in fact, team members have acknowledged in retrospect that extra efforts in difficult situations are the very factors which bind them more closely together. Lastly, in an effort to more normalize the weekend, a special attempt has been made to use facilities not specifically designed for the physically disabled.

## FUND RAISING

The HEC weekend is supported entirely from donations. No candidate is asked to pay any part of the weekend. HEC is not tax exempt nor is it incorporated. This is purposely the case. HEC relies completely on the Christian community for its very existence. Donations come in such forms as time, energy, money, food and personal service.

Money donations come from a variety of sources: team members, former participants, raffles of turkeys and baskets of "cheer". Sometimes donations come from unknown individuals and organizations. Because the general cost of a weekend approximates two thousand dollars, the HEC program is challenged to meet the expenses for rent, medical supplies, and the liturgical items for each weekend.

Supplies are generally solicited by individual team members through hours of work and begging. That which is donated to HEC is freely given, most often, unrecognized. Some formalized attempts to solicit funds have been in letter form, bake sales, garage sales, etc. The genuine generosity of the community at large has thus helped all the retreats meet expenses.

In considering HEC's monetary needs it is important to keep in mind that the purpose of HEC is not to own property, or build a sound financial base from which paid staff can market a product called HEC. HEC tries to keep in mind the Gospel call to "consider the lilies" while at the same time allowing each weekend to generate its own flavor and uniqueness.

Therefore, it is important to re-emphasize that although some general ideas are included in this paper, they are by no means expected to give a guaranteed formula to produce the product HEC. Other HEC programs may find becoming incorporated and/or tax exemption to be very beneficial to their needs. However, the Gospel seems to shout the need that Christians must be fools and trust without fear.

> ... Look how the wild flowers grow; they don't work or make clothes for themselves. But I tell you that not even Solomon, as rich as he was, had clothes as beautiful as one of these flowers. It is God who clothes the wild grass—grass that is here today, gone tomorrow, burned up in the oven. Won't he be all the more sure to clothe you? How little faith you have! So don't be all upset, always concerned about what you will eat and drink. (For the heathen of this world are always concerned about all these things.) Your Father knows that you need these things. Instead, be concerned with his Kingdom, and he will provide you with these things.[10]

Donations of any sort are never refused. If supplies of food or extra money is received that cannot be used in the HEC program, then it is rechanneled directly to the poor or to agencies who support the poor.

---

10 Luke 12:27-31 (*Good News for Modern Man*).

260

## POST HEC EXPERIENCE

The HEC experience has been so powerful that follow-up to the weekend is almost demanded. The experience of coming together and sharing lives for four days becomes such a moving force in the lives of the participants that to limit by stopping contact with the weekend experience itself is impossible.

After each retreat a planned day-long reunion is held which serves as a time to renew friendships, share experiences since the initial retreat, worship together, and continue spiritually growing through these added experiences. Anyone who has ever participated in any of the HECs is invited to participate in any reunion.

Another avenue of follow-up, particularly for those people confined to institutions, is to invite those individuals to participate in more than one retreat. Because of the lack of mobility facing most disabled people, an alternative small group meeting has been encouraged in central geographic locations. These groups meet at either a local church hall or someone's home to share their daily experiences and pray together.

Small groups of HECers also frequently meet for purely social reasons. These social gatherings foster a broadened base for new friendships both for disabled and nondisabled.

For those who are able to write or type, but who cannot be mobile enough to go to meetings, "pen friends" have been suggested. "Pen friends" are prisoners in the New York State Correctional Facilities and old folks across the country. The telephone also plays an extremely important part in intercommunication within the HEC community.

In order to keep everybody abreast of happenings and ideas, three newsletters have been instituted. In the Washington, D.C. area the letter is called *"Heclings."* *"What The HEC"* is in Tuscon. In the New York area the paper is called *"The HECler."*

The newsletters are designed not only to impart information, but also to provide a vehicle of expression for any HECer. The handicapped serve as reporters in general geographic areas to collect information, organize and write columns which are forwarded to central locations where they are typed, printed and distributed.

Periodic renewal weekends specifically designed for only those who have made the HEC weekend are also part of the HEC program. Because of the previously mentioned needs for positive self-image among physically disabled, a major theme for the first renewal weekend is self-image. The need for a specific emphasis in a renewal weekend should grow from the needs of the HEC community and should stress in some way further independence and greater involvement in self-destiny as well as responsibility in the growth of others. One weekend in each year's schedule should be set aside for this renewal experience.

It is easy to see that a post HEC experience is of extreme importance to all members of the HEC community. The opportunity to see one another again, to continue growth in Christianity, and to become more aware of self and others, seems vital to the needs of the physically disabled.

## SUMMARY

This chapter has attempted to describe the program HEC (Handicapped Encounter Christ), and to, in some way determine its effect on the lives of the participants. The program has been explained in some detail and the reasons for its beginning have been discussed.

The evidence points toward continuation of the HEC idea. The format and the forms will, and must, change as HEC revitalizes itself and continues to grow. It would appear, however, that the basic ideas and thrust of HEC—the positive recognition of the worth of each life, will continue. It seems that a program designed for disabled excluding nondisabled and the religious aspects of this weekend, would be out of balance, and therefore, not dealing with the whole being.

It also seems important to realize that the many pages written for this work cannot fully express the feeling and "dynamic" that is the experience of HEC. HEC has become much more than a retreat program, a way of life, or an experiential learning situation. It has become for so many so much a part of each person's self that it is integrated into the total fiber of his or her life. HEC is no longer under control—nor should it be. HEC simply, like life itself, is.

Anyone interested in more details about any aspect of the HEC program may obtain them by contacting:

> Mr John Keck
> Turkey Farm
> Spring Valley Road
> Ossining, New York 19562
> 914-941-8688

# 16
# Becoming
# Yourself

In explaining the role of the TEC weekend in the religious development of the adolescent, Fr. Fedewa insists that the encounter is pre-evangelization. Through the new insights that come from meeting oneself, others and God in a totally different way—a retreat experience—the teenager is disposed to hear the good news.

From my own experience in coordinating TEC follow-up in New York and in teaching senior religion I have been convinced of the importance of a sound and attractive religion program designed to capitalize on the disposition created on the TEC weekend. The following course outline and lesson suggestions were composed for that very purpose.

It is only one of the many possible programs which could successfully "follow-up" a TEC experience. It draws on much of the TEC philosophy and is presently being used with students who will make the weekend sometime during the course. Whether TEC is a pre-requisite, a mid-year experience or a climax to this course should be the decision of those giving the program. They alone can judge by observation and prayer what would be most beneficial and possible for their group.

It is a step in evangelization. As such it begins in the daily experiences of relationships and builds to the announcement of the friendship which makes all friendships new: our personal relationship with Jesus Christ. That transforming relationship is then deepened through the reality of the People of God in His Body, the Church.

## COURSE OUTLINE

This is a course which has as its core the realization that Jesus' Paschal Mystery is also the mystery of each human person's search for fulfillment in love of self, love of others and love of God.

*TOPIC 1:* Becoming Yourself with others and with yourself.

*AIM:* In the same way that Jesus comes to us in flesh, we try to discover in human relationships the Paschal struggles of doubt, risk, trust and mistrust, acceptance and rejection.

267

*MATERIALS:*

Readings: Bach, Richard. *Jonathan Livingston Seagull*
Paulus, Trina. *Hope for the Flowers*.

Films: "Marty" screenplay by Paddy Chayevsky *United Artists*, Helen Keller, United Artists *Alabare*, Charismatic Renewal Services

\* Exercises: Shield
tombstone
relatiogram

\* Prayer experiences: God as Loving Father

*METHODS:* Class presentation, discussion, group work and work in pairs are used to examine the variety of materials for the relationship steps of doubt, risk, trust/mistrust and acceptance/rejection. Application of these ideas are then made to the personal lives of those in the course.

*EVALUATION* (*optional*): a three page paper tracing an important theme through "Marty," "Helen Keller," *Hope for the Flowers, Jonathan Livingston Seagull* and the student's own lives.

*OVERVIEW:* It is important to note that the psychological point of view taken on this topic is the molding of a clay form. There is no life without the breath of God. From the very beginning the team offering this course must realize the need

---

\* See detailed explanation of exercises and prayer experiences at the end of the lesson suggestions.

for this indwelling of the Spirit. Class prayer, personal witness and opportunities for religious experience are an essential part of this course.

The real relationship which will transform relationships with self and others is the personal relationship with Jesus Christ. The experience of the stages of relationship—doubt, risk, trust/mistrust, acceptance/rejection on the human level is simply a way of preparing for the realization of God's unconditional acceptance of us and the intimate friendship with Jesus Christ awaiting us as disciples of Christ.

A weekly team meeting for prayer is crucial to the upbuilding of the teachers offering this course. This prayer time could also be used in part for discussion of course problems and future direction.

*TOPIC 2:* Becoming yourself by forming a lifestyle.

*AIM:* Maturity is achieved only as a person becomes more and more integrated. Here the theme of lifestyle is employed to help the student examine other lifestyles and his own lifestyle to understand that the greatest work one will ever do will be the creation of oneself.

The obstacles that life presents which often destroy the lifestyle we are trying to create will also be examined. In this way we will see that the struggle of life is the Paschal Mystery of Jesus.

Ideals clash with reality, hope with despair, dreams with nightmares. The victory or the defeat of our lifestyle depends upon the power that we have to deal effectively with reality. That power is Jesus as the lifestyle is Christ's.

A) Ideals, Hopes and Dreams: The Me I'd Dare to be
B) Reality, Despair and Nightmare: The Struggle
C) The Victory: to be fully human is to be in the light of Jesus Christ

*MATERIALS:*

Readings: Ten Boom, Corrie. *The Hiding Place.*
Thoreau, Henry D. "What I lived for"
Chapter 2, *Walden.*

Records: "Trial of the Catonsville Nine."
"Man of La Mancha" sound track.
Films: Solo, Pyramid Films

*Films,* from Charismatic Renewal Services

Filmstrip: "Sacrament of Reconciliation" by Thos. Klise

Exercises: personal ideal
Christmas cards
Focolare' presentation

Prayer experiences: Penance Service
Sacrament of Reconciliation
Jesus—Friend, Brother, Savior
Christmas Liturgy
Renewal of Baptism Vows

*METHODS:* Class representation, group discussion, meditation.

*EVALUATION* (optional): an objective test on the *Hiding Place* and a three page paper on the themes in the *Hiding Place*.

*TOPIC 3:* Becoming Yourself by meeting Jesus

*AIM:* to discover that the power that brought victory to Corrie Ten Boom in her nightmare can be ours. We need only to grow in our friendship with Jesus.

*MATERIALS:*

Readings: "The Courage to Accept Acceptance"—Chapter 1 of Peter Von Bremmen's *As Bread is Broken*
"Jesus Christ: Madman or Lord" from *New Covenant,* December 1976.
"Breakfast with Jesus" from *New Covenant,* December 1976.
Bible

Films: film from Charismatic Renewal Services narrated by Jim Ferry.

Exercises: God's Shield, ladder of faith

Prayer experience: Holy Spirit: Advocate, Comforter, Power

                    Blessing of Throats
                    Private prayer
                    Prayer with scriptures
                    Eucharist
                    Service of Ashes

*METHOD:* This topic is organized as a four part course in personal relationship with Jesus. God's Love and Salvation are the first two themes and New Life and prayer are the last two. It is an introduction to a prayer relationship—private and group prayer.

*EVALUATION* (*optional*): a 16 day personal prayer log using the 16 chapters in Mark's gospel.

*TOPIC 4:* Becoming Yourself by placing your friendship with Jesus at the core of your personal lives.

*AIM:* This is a three part section which helps the student see how friendship with Jesus can help achieve victory in our personal lives—victory over guilt, fear and loneliness—that is over sin, suffering and death.

Section one deals with our friendship with ourselves in the light of Jesus. Section two deals with friendship with others, dating, marriage and other life decisions in the light of Jesus. In the third section the student takes a deeper look at

his or her friendship with Jesus through meditation, private prayer and group prayer.

This victory over guilt, fear and loneliness
through forgiveness, the gifts of the Holy Spirit
and God's transforming presence brings this topic
to a conclusion and opens up the final topic of
Becoming Yourself in the Body of Christ.


*MATERIALS:*

Readings: Trobisch, Walter, *I loved a Girl*
Marriage Encounter Series
Lange and Cushing. *Healing and Free-
dom,* Chapter 1
Linn and Linn. *Healing of Memories*
Exercises
Doherty, Catherine. "You are an Image
of God" from *New Covenant.* May 1977
Abbot David Gaeret, "Pentecostalism:
Trinitarian Perspective" from *Catholic
Charismatic,* Nov. '76

Film: "The Story of Eric" or "Becoming" (Natural
Childbirth films)

Prayer experiences: Healing of Memories

Exercises: Role Playing

Speakers: Vocation talks on the meaning of priest-
hood, brotherhood, sisterhood and marriage.


*METHOD:* Class presentation, group work, speakers and exercises.

273

*EVALUATION (optional)*: Objective Test on *I Loved a Girl*. Three letters by the student answering some of the problems of Francoise and Cecile in *I Loved a Girl*.


*TOPIC 5*: Becoming Yourself in the Body of Christ

*AIM*: The final topic is designed like the final day of TEC to be an opening outward of the personal relationship with Jesus. The reality of the Pentecost experience is that relationship with Jesus must have a communal dimension to be genuine. The community of believers is nourished by the sacraments and expresses itself by Christian action.


*MATERIALS:*

Readings: Scanlan, Michael. "Emmaus, Model for Encountering Jesus in the Sacraments" from *Catholic Charismatic*, July-August 1976.

Films: *The Hiding Place* from Billy Graham, Minnesota
*Decision at Delano* (United Farm Workers)

Prayer experiences: Confirmation Renewal
personal witness of young people in community


*METHOD*: Class presentations, group discussion

274

*EVALUATION:* Sacramental Autobiography: telling your life story through the sacraments. What it meant at the time, What it means now. Using pictures and words.

Lesson Suggestions: These brief lesson suggestions are obviously not lesson plans. They are meant only as theme statements to begin the planning of a class by the only person who can presume to do that—the course teacher. They are designed for a full year religion course in a school using a six day rotating cycle, during which fifty-minute religion classes meet twice a cycle.

## EXERCISES AND PRAYER EXPERIENCES

This explanation is a brief catalogue of some of the experiences that have worked with high school students.

*RELATIOGRAM:* Each student is told to draw a full page circle. At the center of the circle, a small circle containing the word, "me", is written. The class is then broken up into pairs, circles are exchanged and in the form of an interview the couples chart each others 6-10 closest relationships on the circle. The closer a person is, the closer that person is placed to the center, "Me".

It should look something like this.

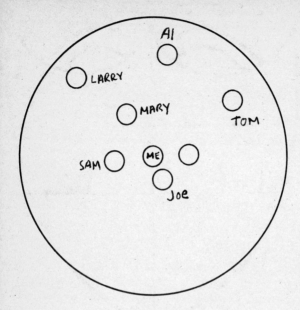

Circles are returned after the interview and the following analysis is done. 1) List the percentage of same sex relationships, 2) opposite sex, 3) family members, 4) what makes the difference between farthest and closest?, 5) Was I the initiator of the closest relationship?, 6) List the amount of time you have known each person. Is there a pattern? rising order? falling order?

Later in the course, you can return to this relatiogram to see the stages of relationships in the chart.

SHIELD: This is an identity exercise that is widely used. The students are given blank coat of arms. They must fill in each of the sections with a picture symbolizing their answer.

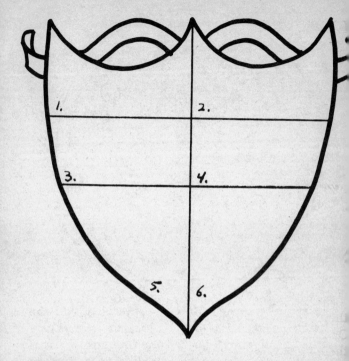

1) My best quality
2) My greatest accomplishment
3) My family's greatest accomplishment
4) My worst failure
5) What my parents think of me
6) What my friends think of me
7) My three word motto

At the completion of this, the class is broken up
into groups of four to explain their answers. The
groups upon completion are combined and the
explanation is repeated until the class is in one
big circle and all can see and hear each person's
explanation. This may take 2 classes.

## TOMBSTONES:

The students are given two blank tombstones and they are asked to write 2 epitaphs for themselves. One is to be their *desired* epitaph. The other is their *probable* epitaph. This can be shared in groups or as one class.

An interesting angle to take is to observe the differences and formulate *concrete* resolutions to make the probable become the desired.

## PRAYER EXPERIENCE OF GOD AS FATHER:

Using music and directive prayer, groups can be exposed to God and prayer without the pressure of a reaction. These can be easily put together from contemporary religious music, bible readings and improvising by the leader. Here is a sample program.

"Slow down," a song by Chuck Girard put to a slide show.

Reading from 1 John 3, leader's comments—we are the children of ABBA.

"Be Not Afraid," a song from the album *Earthen Vessels* by the St. Louis Jesuits, reading Isaiah 40 leader's comment: meditative thoughts on strength that comes from being loved.

"I will never forget you," the title song from Carey Landry's album. Silent Petitions.

## CIRCLE OF MY LIFE:

On a circle, divide your life into four sections:

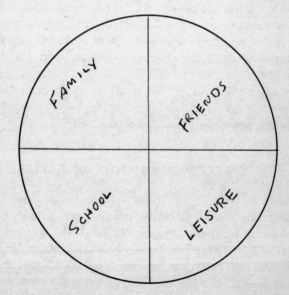

Then, divide sections into subdivisions:

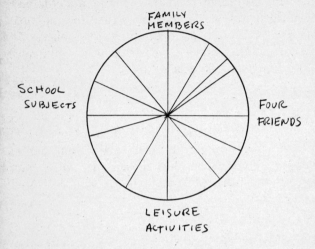

Then, for each subdivision i.e., relationship, activity etc. list one constructive thing you are doing now toward building up that aspect, one destructive thing you are doing now to hurt that aspect and one specific resolution toward improving that aspect.


*PERSONAL IDEAL:*


A take-home exercise in which the student chooses a person from history, literature, film or their own experience who they would choose to admire and to imitate. This should be prepared on an index card to be presented to class. It should contain a brief identification of the person and a description of what it is they admire about the person.

*CHRISTMAS CARDS:* It probably hasn't happened for a number of years that the students were encouraged to make a Christmas card for their parents. It is really an exercise in expressiveness. The written medium makes it easier to say what many have often wanted to say.

*FOCOLARE':* The Focolare' community is always eager to spread their warm understanding of the Christian message. It fits well here as another example of someone who has chosen an ideal. I would suggest that the presentations be done in small groups.

*JESUS-PRAYER EXPERIENCE*—choose songs and scripture texts as in the first experience to lead prayer around the idea of Jesus as friend, brother and Savior. Suggestions: John's last discourse, Paul's letter to the Romans, Chapter 8; songs: James Taylor's "You've Got A Friend," Neil Diamond's "He's Not Heavy, He's My Brother," Carey Landry's "Brother Jesus," Simon and Garfunkel's "Bridge Over Trouble Waters."

*GOD'S SHIELD:*

Like the personal coat of arms, this exercise helps in making concrete the student's present picture of God. The questions here are: 1) God's best quality, 2) God's greatest accomplishment, 3) a time when I felt God failed me, 4) God's picture of me, 5) my present relationship with God, 6) my future relationship with God, 7) God's motto.

*LADDER OF FAITH:* There are often many barriers that keep us from taking a risk of faith. On a five-rung ladder have the students list some of the times they have felt abandoned by God. Then, have them try to think of some of the good that may have risen out of that problem. Then in a few moments of silent prayer direct them as they "climb over" these obstacles and take the risk of trusting.

*HOLY SPIRIT PRAYER SERVICE:* This is the third prayer reflection on the Trinity. Here the Holy Spirit is encountered as Advocate, Comforter and Giver of Gifts.

Suggestions: Genesis creation story, Ezekiel 37, Acts 2

Songs: "Song of New Life" by Carey Landry, "Spirit of the Living God," Word of Life Records.

*HEALING OF MEMORIES*—see book by that title by Matthew and Dennis Lynn. There are five exercises on forgiveness in the back of the book.

## LESSON SUGGESTIONS

Cycle 1:  Theme: a) Becoming Yourself: introduction to course and to each other.

             Materials: a brief course outline
                     b) Relatiogram

Cycle 2:  a) Doubt, Risk, Trust/Mistrust, Acceptance/Rejection: 4 stages of relationships
            b) "Marty" (film)

Cycle 3:  a) film discussion
            b) Relationship stages on "Marty"

Cycle 4:  a) *Jonathan Livingston Seagull* Reading Day with background music from album
            b) Personal Shield

Cycle 5:  a) "Helen Keller" film
            b) film discussion

Cycle 6: a) *Hope for the Flowers*—reading class
—aloud in class
b) Relationship stages in book

Cycle 7: a) God as Father, Prayer Experience
b) evaluation of prayer experience—
doubt, risk, trust and acceptance of
prayer.

Cycle 8: a) Quiz on *Jonathan*
(Optional) b) brainstorm, ideas for evaluation
prayer
(Topic 2)

Cycle 9: a) Personal Ideals—introduce
b) Personal Ideals—present

Cycle 10: a) Ideals—Hopes—Dreams: the Me I'd
dare to be—"Man of La Mancha"
b) Ideals: Thoreau's "What I lived for"

Cycle 11: a) forming a lifestyle means creating
yourself. Introduce circle of life.
b) Circle of Life

Cycle 12: a) Ideals lead to suffering: Corrie Ten
Boom, Don Quixote, Jesus
b) Ideals/Reality; Dreams/Nightmares;
Hope/Despair.

Cycle 13: a) "Solo"—film
b) discussion of film

Cycle 14: a) Quiz on *Hiding Place*/discussion
b) discussion on *Hiding Place*

Cycle 15: a) The Victory: to be fully human (to
be fulfilled, to become myself, to be

285

happy) I need to be in the light of Christ: John's Gospel: Samaritan Woman, Nicodemus, Zaccheus, Adulteress

b) Focolare Presentation

Cycle 16: a) Focolare Discussion
b) Prayer experience II: Jesus

Cycle 17: a) Brainstorming for Project on *Hiding Place*
b) Project work Period

Cycle 18: a) Becoming Yourself by meeting Jesus
(Topic 3)

Jesus' Shield

b) The courage to accept acceptance God's Love

Cycle 19: a) Ladder of faith
b) "Jesus: Madman or Lord?" Salvation

Cycle 20: a) Preparation for Sacrament of Reconciliation Thomas Klise filmstrip
b) Sacrament of Reconciliation

Cycle 21: a) Breakfast with Jesus—personal relationship
b) Prayer Experience  3: The Holy Spirit

Cycle 22: a) Becoming Yourself by making Jesus the core of your personal life: Pentecostalism: Trinitarian Perspectives

(Topic 4)
Assign
*I Loved a Girl*

b) "You are the Image of God" by Catherine Doherty

Cycle 23:  a) Quiz/Discussion: *I Loved a Girl*
               b) Discussion: *I Loved a Girl.*

Cycle 24:  a) Life Choices: Marriage, Marriage Encounter Series 1, 4, 7, 8
               b) Marriage: Marriage Encounter Series 2, 3, 6, 9, 11

Cycle 25:  a) Marriage: Marriage Encounter Series 12, 13, 14
               b) "Becoming" a natural childbirth film

Cycle 26:  Religious Vocation: What is a Sister?

               a) presentation
               b) film/discussion

Cycle 27:  What is a Brother?
               a) presentation
               b) film/discussion

Cycle 28:  What is a Priest?

               a) presentation
               b) film/discussion

Cycle 29:  The Single Life

               a) presentation
               b) film/discussion

Cycle 30:  Friendship with Jesus

               a) "Encountering Jesus in the Sacraments"
               b) Graduation Prayer Service

## CONCLUSION

Catechists will always differ on the right way to announce the good news and to nurture the growth of the seed of faith. This brief presentation of a course outline and lesson suggestions is an attempt at bringing the student into a deeper awareness of his faith through a personal encounter with his Savior, Jesus Christ. In religious education, we have very limited time with our students; we are opposed on all sides by the anti-christian world around us. This is my choice of what is the best to give them in light of the obstacle of time and the opponents of an anti-religious world. It will not be for every program. However, like the TEC weekend, I believe it is an experience in the resounding of the gospel which is sound in content and adapted to the culture of the students. Also like the TEC weekend the key to this, or any attempt at religious education for that matter, is the realization that content and culture are the things which *God* employs to show Himself to His loved ones. It is our dependence on Him in prayer, personal witnessing and stepping out in faith that transforms the work of our hands. He alone changes hearts and we will be instruments in His hands when our hearts are converted daily.

*Note:* This course has been, and is being, successfully taught. Anyone interested in more details about any aspect of this course may obtain them by contacting:

> Mr. Thomas Rogers
> Sacred Heart High School
> 34 Convent Ave.
> Yonkers, New York 10703.

All books and audiovisual materials here described are obtainable from Alba House Communications, Canfield, Ohio, 44406.

I Will Search at Odd Angles

James Goedken

Prayers for all Occasions

Father James Goedken in *I Will Search at Odd Angles* (Alba Books, $1.75) presents us with a free-form prayer book for high school students. Goedken works with teenagers in Cedar Rapids, Iowa. His prayers are couched in the language and ideas of that group. They concern the problems of teenagers. The publisher assures us that these prayers have been effectively used. There cannot, of course, be any guarantee of effectiveness but I was impressed by the book. The style is easy and familiar and mercifully free of jargon. Each prayer is anchored by a scriptural quotation which powerfully echoes and reiterates the theme of the prayer.

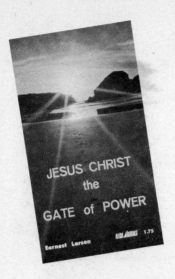